Morning Mercies

365 Poems to Celebrate God's Love

I pray you enjoy reading this book of poetry as much as I enjoyed writing it.

In Christ Love,
Patsy

Patsy Bunton

Lamentations 3:22-

Morning Mercies: 365 Poems to Celebrate God's Love

Copyright 2019 Patsy Bunton

All Rights Reserved

ISBN: 978-1-940645-64-3

Greenville, South Carolina

Printed in the United States of America

Dedication

This book is dedicated to my grandson, Seth Oswald, who is the inspiration for these poems. In 2015, Seth's mom gave me a journal as a Christmas gift, and each day over the next year I wrote a poem for my grandson. Here is the note I wrote to him at the beginning of my journal:

When God takes me home to heaven, I pray you will take this journal and read it often. When God allows you to become a father, I pray you will read it and pass it on to your family. Remember: The words I write come from God — He alone inspires me. Always "let your light so shine before men that they may see your good works and glorify your Father in heaven" (Matthew 5:16).

All my love,
GaGa

Acknowledgments

First, to God the Father, Jesus Christ my Savior, and the Holy Spirit who inspires me to write poetry: I acknowledge You!

Then, there are two very special women in my life I wish to acknowledge. One is the lady who found my lost journal of poetry, Kathy Bird Spivey. The other is our church's executive secretary, Mary Lou Ridenour, who lovingly typed the pages of this book in order for me to prepare it for the publisher. I love you both dearly.

Last, but certainly not least, I must thank my husband, Kirby, who attempts to punctuate my poetry correctly.

Without all of you, this book would never have become a reality. Thank you from the bottom of my heart.

Lovingly,
Patsy

January 1

A New Beginning

When I awoke this morning,
A new year had begun;
A year of special memories
Given to me by God's Son.

A new year, a new beginning:
What will God have in store?
I'm excited to discover what blessings
He just keeps giving more and more.

I'm praying for more holiness,
For health and happiness, too.
Oh, the joy that fills my life
When I see the things He'll do.

Let each day be a new beginning;
Read God's Word and earnestly pray.
There are so many rewards awaiting
If we just seize the day!

January 2

FEISTY FAITH

Don't ever be afraid
To show your feisty faith.
It makes God chuckle.
He thinks it is great.

You make up your mind
To never, ever quit.
No matter what opposition,
You use your quick wit

To stop the biggest bully,
Making insecurity fly out the door;
Knowing you'll have victory,
For you know God has so much more

Power He will give you,
And it won't ever be late.
Embrace His grace and mercy,
And use your Feisty Faith!

January 3

USE ME

Use me, dear Lord,
This very day
To touch some soul
And lead the way

For them to know
You will carry their cross.
It does not matter
The time or loss.

For He is ready;
He awaits your call.
The burden never too large
Or never too small.

So use me, dear Lord,
Today, is my plea
To direct someone,
Dear Father, to Thee.

Use me!

January 4

THE QUIET NIGHT

The quiet night
Gives time to reflect
On what we've done
Or what did we neglect.

We wonder in our minds
Where did the day go?
There was so much to do,
So much more to know.

Our eyes grow heavy,
Our body longs for sleep,
But minds just won't rest
Thinking too deep.

Yet, the quiet nights
Will eventually turn to rest.
We bow our heads in prayer.
Thank You, God … we're so blessed.

January 5

HE DELIGHTS IN YOU

He delights in you,
So make Him proud.
Let all those you meet
Know without a doubt

God is in control
Of what happens each day;
So live it to the fullest,
But live it in His way.

Be strong and of good courage;
Let the whole world see
The Master of the Universe
Alive in you and me.

He delights in you,
So don't let Him down.
He is tenderly watching;
In Him, true Joy is found.

January 6

SING OF GOD'S MERCY

Sing of God's mercy
At the dawn of the day.
Be thankful and praise Him
In work and in play.

When noontime arrives,
Give Him glory again,
The middle of the day
Looking forward to the end.

Rejoice at five o'clock;
The world looks so bright,
Evening is drawing near,
Soon will come the night.

As we lie down to rest,
Sing of His mercy once more,
And be grateful; fall asleep,
Looking forward to what He has in store.

January 7

GIVE ME JOY

Happiness is external;
Joy comes from deep within.
The love of Jesus Christ
Is where it all begins.

Happiness will fade;
Joy will still abound,
For it comes from the soul
Where true joy is found.

Father, give me joy;
Give me happiness, too.
All my life I dedicate
Totally to You.

Let my joy spread
To my family and friends,
And help them pass it on,
So my joy will never end.

January 8

Today I Will Sing

Today I will sing
Though troubles surround,
For in Jesus, my Savior,
True hope is found.

I'll give Him my burdens
For in Him I find rest.
The faith He has given
Will carry me through each test.

I'll pray for the answers
To whatever befalls;
His ears are forever listening
Whenever I call.

So, today I will sing,
My voice lifted in praise.
God carries my burdens
All my nights and my days.

January 9

Outside My Window

Outside my window
I see a squirrel at play.
I think how wonderful
To start off any day.

Full of vim and vigor
Exploring everything around,
This small animal
Scurrying across the ground.

I watch it grab an acorn,
Hide it away, then look for more.
So busy and industrious,
I wonder what else it might store.

I thank God for His creation,
For joy in watching a squirrel.
There are so many blessings
In His marvelous world.

January 10

WEALTHY PAUPERS

Are you a wealthy pauper?
Do your blessings go unseen
Because you chose the world
And the things you could glean?

Have you found the purpose
God has for your life?
Or do you live in poverty,
Knowing nothing but strife?

Do you know of God's provisions,
Riches far beyond this earth?
God our Father, God our Son, and God our Holy Spirit
Has given us from our birth.

Chosen by God the Father;
Predestined us in His will;
Oh, the love He's shown
And His mercy instilled.

God's precious Son redeemed us;
His blood flowed from you and me;
His forgiveness of our trespasses
Hung on Calvary's tree.

January 10

God the Holy Spirit sealed us;
He works in our lives each day;
We have ownership of salvation.
At the feet of God, we lay

Our very being,
Deposited and secure,
Assured of our heavenly home,
Our bodies, whole and new.

So if you feel like a pauper,
Meet God and turn around.
You will become a wealthy soul,
For only in Him can true wealth be found.

January 11

Today's Grace

Lord, today I'll walk in Your grace
Knowing You hold on to me,
Knowing I can face
Whatever the day may bring.

I find strength in your promises,
Shelter within your arms.
Your mercy abounds;
Your glory surrounds.

Doubts flee from my mind,
Filled with Your love divine.
May I let you alone shine;
I know You are mine.

So, Lord, today I'll walk in grace.
No fear, no regrets.
Plunging forward in today
By faith … believing … receiving.

January 12

Today I'll Walk

Today I'll walk
Where Jesus asks;
I won't shirk my duty
Whatever the task.

My body weary,
My soul ablaze;
I'll honor Him,
I'll give Him praise.

The day is young.
What will it bring?
I only know
My heart must sing,

For today I'll walk
As I try each day,
With my hand in His,
Letting Him lead the way.

January 13

WALK BLESSED

Release your faith,
Let it fly.
Let your heart ring
Till it reaches the sky.

Surround yourself
With Christian friends,
So together you shine
Showing love without end.

Discover a new vision
For the future … then
Ask God for help.
He'll supply it when …

You give Him your all.
Walk blessed each day,
For the Master of the Universe
Will lead your way.

January 14

A GLIMPSE OF GLORY

As the sun rises,
May I always see
A glimpse of Glory
Allowing me to be

Awakened, refreshed,
My soul afire.
Starting my day
With a holy desire

To be all I can be,
To do all I can do.
Connected to the power source;
God … that is You!

Possessing an understanding
That can only increase,
And my day will end
In His perfect peace.

January 15

Lazy Days

I thank the Lord
For lazy days:
Rain pelting on the windows;
A gray winter haze.

A time to reflect
In the week almost gone,
Thinking how precious
Each day has grown.

All the years behind me,
A new year in store;
What could one ask for,
Except for more

Time to make memories
To store in our hearts each day,
For lazy days reminiscing
When it's too wet to go out and play.

January 16

WORRIES AND CONCERNS

Worries and concerns
Fly out the door.
God will make a way;
He sends blessings galore.

Just when doubt enters,
Call out His name.
He'll change your attitude,
Your anxieties tame.

For God gives you faith
To know His Word is true.
He always keeps His promises;
He will never forsake you.

So grasp hold of His hand.
Hold on really tight.
Give God your worries and concerns;
He makes all things right.

January 17

Wherever My Feet Lead Me

Wherever my feet
Lead me today,
I'll choose the path
As God leads the way.

I'll smile at someone
Or shake someone's hand,
Or wish someone well
As God commands.

I'll live in joy
As the day will progress.
And when nightfall comes,
I'll find sweet rest.

So, wherever my feet
Lead me today,
I'll touch another soul,
Dear Lord, I pray.

January 18

BLESSED TO BE A BLESSING

Blessed to be a blessing,
That's what God says to me:
All that I have given you
I want you to use, you see,

To help another soul,
Feel the strength and power
I have given to you
At just the right hour.

I want you to be a light
Along life's darkened pathway,
To shine on someone else
Each and every day.

For I've blessed you to be a blessing,
To come along with Me,
To use what I have given you,
To help someone else find victory.

January 19

Battles We Must Face

There are battles we must face
Each and every day,
Battles often unforeseen
That haunt us along life's way.

We need the armor of God's Word
To give us courage and strength,
To plunge headlong and fast,
To go to any length

To win the battle, fighting hard,
To grasp what we must do;
To always persevere in trials,
Knowing, Lord, we can count on You.

So, help us in our daily walk
To find Your wisdom great.
For our lives are in Your hands;
You know what will be our fate.

January 20

MOTIVATED

Let me be motivated
Today, dear Lord, I pray.
Keep my mind focused
In my work and play.

Let my eyes see
What You would have me do,
As I journey on the path
Selected, Father, by You.

Let my feet walk
The path You chose.
Keep me from stumbling,
Your will not to oppose.

I want to do my very best
In all I need to do:
Motivated, inspired,
Living life anew.

January 21

NEW LIFE

"What are you searching for?"
Is the question for today.
Is it peace, joy and happiness?
What stands in your way?

Life is so very precious,
A gift from God above;
The wonders of His mercy
Steeped in His deep love.

You can start a "new life";
The old one you can shed.
Just trust in the Living Word;
On it, you can be fed.

Bringing forth something marvelous
For you to truly enjoy
A new life in the Father:
Receive it, then employ!

January 22

Make This Day Count

Outside the sky is gray,
The wind is blowing strong.
No sunshine to be found;
The day may seem forlorn.

But inside there is warmth
And light for us to see,
So we can make this day count
If our hearts are filled with glee.

Each day is a special gift,
Though outside it seems not so.
For winter's chill has settled in,
But spring comes soon, we know.

So make this day count
And every day hereafter.
God is in control;
Fill your days with laughter.

January 23

Blanket of Snow

Today a blanket of snow
Lays on the ground;
Its beauty unsurpassed
As you look all around.

It won't last here long
As the temperature begins to rise,
But I am so thankful
To wake up to such a surprise.

God's handiwork is marvelous,
Unlike that of human man;
Each season of the year
Flows by at His command.

I bow my head in thankfulness
For all that He supplies,
As the beautiful blanket of snow
Disappears from our eyes.

January 24

God's Mercy Is Abundant

God's mercy is abundant;
We see it every day.
He extends to us blessings
All along life's way.

We arise in the morning,
Seeing His glory abound.
The beauty of the sun
In the sky is found.

He carries us through the day
And gives us rest at night;
Renewing us once again
To face the morning light.

His mercies so abundant,
May we always remember to say:
Thank You, Heavenly Father,
At the beginning of each day.

January 25

AWAKEN TO WORSHIP

Awaken to worship.
God brought you through the night.
Open your eyes in amazement
At dawn's early light.

The moon is still shining,
Ushering in the day.
Arise and be gladdened
As you kneel to pray.

Spend the day rejoicing;
Be thankful in all things,
Looking forward with anticipation
To what the day may bring.

So, awaken to worship.
Let joy fill your soul.
A new day has begun.
Be excited to see how it unfolds.

January 26

A Special Place

There's a special place
For each of us to be:
A place of perfect peace,
A place of harmony.

A place where we find comfort
Or joy within the day,
Whether we are very busy
Or just a day to play.

Every day is important,
So live it, my friend, with zest.
Be kind to others
In your daily quest.

For God has a special place
For each of us to be:
A place of perfect peace,
A place of harmony.

January 27

USE YOUR LIFE

Use your life;
Don't waste it
On worldly things,
My friend.
So much more is waiting
Just around the bend.

God's promises are real;
Seek Him and find
True joy from within
Your body, soul, and mind.
So much more is waiting
He wants you to find

How to use your life,
To serve wherever you are found,
Truly understanding
Life's circle going 'round.
Making the most of life
Before you are heaven-bound.

January 28

Today I Release My Cares

Today I release my cares
To the Mighty Father above,
The One who knows me best,
Who showers me with love.

Whatever comes my way,
Whatever the day may bring,
I'll cherish it to my best
And give praise to my King.

Though dark and gloomy outside,
Within my heart there's a glow,
Knowing what is meant to be
Will before my eyes unfold.

So, today I release my cares.
No worry in me will be found;
I've turned it over to the Master
Who has set me on solid ground.

January 29

WASTING TIME

Wasting time, we think,
Is waiting for someone
To show up for a set time
But knowing it won't be done.

Wasting time, we think,
Is when our project falls apart,
Working on it so diligently
And then losing heart.

Wasting time, we think,
Is stopping what we're doing to be
A loving, patient grandparent.
But all too soon to see

We weren't wasting time;
We were making memories to share
When we are old and gray,
And those grandchildren are no longer there.

So don't ever waste your time,
But use it, and if plans fall through,
Realize it was meant to be;
It was what God had planned for you.

January 29

Time is a precious commodity.
"Wasting time" can be, too.
When it's spent with family and friends,
You'll discover this is true.

There is no "Wasting Time."

January 30

Mountains and Valleys

Sometimes we're on a mountaintop,
Sometimes in a valley deep.
But the Master of the Universe
Is always there to keep

Us on the path to safety
With tender love and care.
Sheltering us in His arms,
Our Father is always there.

Some days seem so gloomy,
Others filled with sheer delight.
That's when the Lord is nearest,
Showering us in His light.

So when the highest mountain
Appears before our eyes,
Store up those precious moments.
A valley may be looming nearby.

January 31

Our Church's Vision

It takes God's people
To help a vision grow.
It takes the Master
To help us to show

How to be a disciple
Who disciples someone new.
That should be our desire,
And it takes me and you

To fulfill this vision.
We must implement
A strategic plan
That God has sent.

Everyone needs to be involved;
We all have a special place.
The Father has ordained us
By His amazing grace.

If we are to grow,
Each one has a part
In the greater vision,
Deep down in our heart.

January 31

We must pray for God's will,
Then listen when He speaks.
Put words into action.
Get busy and seek

Those who have strayed,
Those who are lost.
It's not an easy task,
But consider the cost.

It may take change
Or hardships along the way,
But we must stand strong
Each and every day.

We must bring God glory
In all we do.
As we implement our vision,
It takes more than a few.

So, get on board, God's people.
Help our vision to grow.
The Master's wisdom is with us.
Watch Him put on a show!

January 31

Go forward with boldness;
Let faith take control.
Let Corinth Baptist Church's
Implemented vision unfold.

February 1

Let Joy Abound

A new month has begun;
May you let joy abound.
There's beauty everywhere
If you just look around.

The sun shines with splendor,
The pines stand erect and tall,
The rye grass of winter …
Our Heavenly Father made them all.

As season flows into season,
Each has its special perks.
We look forward to each one,
Different looks in the works.

But joy should truly reign
In our hearts each day,
As the Master of the Universe
His majesty displays.

February 2

The Day Has Begun

The day has begun:
What challenges will we meet?
What encounters will be there
For our day to greet?

Will our day be busy,
Or a day to relax?
Will there be joy,
Or will it be taxed?

The Father knows each moment,
How our day will go,
Whether it be fast-paced
Or really, really slow.

Our day has begun.
Let's live it to the fullest,
Making this very day
One of our coolest.

February 3

A Song in My Heart

The winds are howling,
The skies gray and bleak,
But there's a song in my heart;
It's the middle of the week.

When storm clouds rise,
And the rain pelts the ground,
We know there's sunshine
Lurking around.

So make the best
Of every day given.
If tomorrow comes,
And we are still living …

The sun may be shining,
Or the rain may continue,
But there'll be a song in my heart
With a new day's venue.

February 4

Fashioned by God

Each of us is unique,
Fashioned by God above;
Given special talents
By His amazing love.

Each one a different personality,
Maybe a different color of skin,
Made very personable,
But all of us are kin.

We each have relationships
We develop over the years,
Those who share deeply
Their joys and their tears.

Each of us were fashioned
To be who we are
By the Glorious Creator,
Our Bright Morning Star.

February 5

Make Us Your Instrument

The cold winds blow;
The sun shines bright.
Thank You, Father,
For bringing us through the night.

Each day more precious
Than the day before;
Looking forward to seeing
What You have in store.

Give us the strength,
Help us to endure.
Whatever may befall,
Of one thing we are sure:

You'll be beside us,
Leading us today.
"Make us Your instrument,"
This I pray.

February 6

Don't Give Up

Don't give up
On plans you made.
God never gives up on you;
Don't let your plans fade.

There is hope for tomorrow,
A solution around the bend.
So don't give up;
Keep keeping on, my friend.

Just try a little harder;
Help is on the way.
The Father of the Universe
Knows what you need today.

Don't give up.
Just set your mind
To accomplish your plan.
A solution you will find.

February 7

YET ANOTHER DAY

Amid the hustle and bustle
Sunday morning brings,
Our hearts are filled with joy,
A melody to sing.

A new week is beginning;
What will it have in store?
Each day a true blessing,
Receiving more and more

Of God's grace and power,
Being showered with love.
Lifting holy hands,
Giving thanks to God above.

And as the day closes,
Kneeling down to pray,
We thank You, Heavenly Father,
For yet another glorious day.

February 8

Sitting Here Remembering

Sitting here remembering
Days that long ago passed
Brings a smile to my face,
Joys that forever last.

Births of my children,
Of grands and great-grands, too,
Make my heart flutter
Thinking of all we used to do.

Now as I grow older,
I look at pictures and see
How much love was shared
Between them and me.

Age may take away many things,
Maybe even take my mind.
But I pray they cherish
All the memories left behind.

Family get-togethers,
Vacations in the mountains or on shores;
Times of reflecting on
Those memories we have stored.

February 8

Oh, I love reminiscing,
Thinking of "good old times"
When we would laugh and play,
And it didn't cost a dime

To just be sitting and talking
Or snuggling, watching TV.
These are the precious moments
That are dearest to me.

Just sitting here remembering,
Pure joy fills my soul,
As I smile and reflect
On the memories that unfold.

February 9

LIKE JOB, I'D LIKE TO BE

I would like to be
Like Job, you see,
A man God praised
For all of his days.

For Job was righteous,
A man doing good,
Living just like
We all should.

God allowed the devil
To tempt Job day and night;
Job was in torment,
But kept his eye on the Light.

His Savior loved him,
Saw him through each trial.
Though Job was suffering,
He never felt denial.

For he knew God
And cried out in despair.
The Master of the Universe
Was listening with care.

February 9

Knowing that this man
Was great in God's sight
Gives me a reason
To always fight,

To try and become
Like Job in God's eyes;
Winning evil's battle,
The devil's woes deny.

For, like Job,
I'd like to be,
Courageous and unswerving
For all eternity.

February 10

GO AND SHARE

I jumped to my feet
On this brisk, cold morn
Wondering about my day.
Would I end it weary and worn?

Or would I grab hold
Of what the day has in store,
And thank my God
For giving me one more

Day to be thankful
For work and for play,
For all the blessings
He bestows every day?

I'll tackle this brisk morn
And then go and share
This day with some friends,
With love and with care.

February 11

Sitting and Waiting

Sitting and waiting
Seems like a bore.
There's so much to do,
So much in store.

But sit I must
And wait to see
Just what time
My appointment will end up to be.

But there are books,
Or a number of magazines,
Stories and recipes
I can glean.

So sitting and waiting
Isn't so hard.
For a little free time,
I'm actually glad.

February 12

LIVE WITH JOY

Live with joy
Each and every day,
For life is too short
To live any other way.

Keep your chin up,
Even if you feel down;
Something will happen
To turn things around.

Think positively today,
And all your life through;
Somebody special
Has their eyes on you.

So live with joy.
Let love abound.
Life is too short
To wear a frown.

February 13

Bad Days: Goodbye!

Have you ever had a bad day
When everything seemed to go wrong,
But as you reflect back
That day made you strong?

Though things went askew
Not as you planned,
God was in it all;
You felt His mighty hand

Touch you on the cheek,
Saying, "It's all right, my child."
Sometimes troubles hit,
But only for a while.

So, put on a smile;
Your day wasn't a waste.
You plunged full head forward
Without leaving a trace.

You were determined
To leave resentment behind;
Your bad day
Actually turned out fine.

February 13

Bad days turned to glad days;
You can do it if you try.
Just stay courageous and strong;
Kiss those bad days goodbye!

February 14

Say "I Love You"

Say "I love you"
Every day you can,
For tomorrow may not come
And you would have missed your chance

To let someone dear know
How you truly feel.
So grasp the day
And always say "I love you."

Say "I love you,"
For you never know
Who is watching
To see if your love shows.

Let someone dear know
Three simple words:
"I love you!"

February 15

MAKE THE DAY COUNT

Awaken to the aroma
Of coffee brewing nearby,
Starting off the morning
With a stretch and sigh.

Wondering what today holds,
What surprises it might bring
Lifts up your spirit,
Making your heart sing.

Bustling about busily,
Dressing for the day,
Thinking of those you'll meet,
Your heart light and gay.

Make the day count.
Give someone a hug, a smile.
You may be entertaining angels unaware
Even if for a little while.

Make the day count!

February 16

A Promise to Us

The wind is howling,
Ushering in the day.
As leaves dance,
Scurrying to play.

The rains came
During the night,
Cleansing the earth,
To its delight.

A promise to us:
Spring is near
To refresh our spirits,
Our minds to clear

Of the nakedness
And barren land
That will soon spring
To life again.

February 17

Unshakeable

In days of uncertainty,
Lord, let me be
Unshakeable in faith
As I look to Thee.

On my own
I am nothing,
But with You
My heart sings.

Help me to remember
Whatever this day brings;
I know I can make it,
For You are in all things.

Unshakeable I'll stand,
Walking, head up high;
My faith unwavering,
My spirit will fly.

February 18

A Purpose for Today

I woke up this morning,
Wondering in my mind:
What will be my purpose?
What new adventure will I find?

Each day a new beginning,
Goals, hopes and dreams;
Will they become reality?
All too soon, it seems.

What I had intended
Quickly slipped away,
As the day entered,
I thought, "I just want to play."

So my purpose for today
Is to do whatever I can
To put a smile on someone's face,
Or sit and hold my sweetheart's hand.

February 19

ETERNITY CAME FOR HER TODAY

Death waltzed in
With quiet grace;
Life slipped away
Without a trace

Of restlessness
Or regret,
Just one breath,
No fuss or fret.

There was no fight;
Just a little tear
Slid from her eye,
Not a trace of fear.

On angel's wings,
She slipped away.
Eternity came
For her today.

*(Aunt Jimmie died at 11:45 a.m.
as I stood by her bed.)*

February 20

WAKE UP EXPECTANTLY

Wake up expectantly
Of what the day may bring;
Let your spirit soar,
Let your heart sing.

Today may be exciting,
Something new in store.
Something to bring joy
You've never felt before.

Count your many blessings.
Approach life with zest.
We are here for a short time;
Live it to your very best.

When the dark night approaches,
Go to sleep expectantly
To awaken in the morning
Or awaken for eternity.

February 21

A Day Full of Love

Night has fallen;
The day almost spent.
What have you accomplished?
What message have you sent …

To those you were with,
To new people you met?
Think over your day;
Do you have regrets?

I smile and remember
What a wonderful day
With church family and friends,
Pure joy all the way.

As I lay down my head,
I thank God above
For the blessings He gave
With a day full of love.

February 22

When I Awoke

When I awoke
It seemed dark and gloomy,
But in seconds
The sky became bright.

I thanked my Savior
For bringing me
Through the night.

I asked Him for hope;
I asked Him for joy;
I asked Him for peace.
He's given me much more:

A new day to begin,
A new day to laugh, maybe cry,
A new day to discover
The when, the where, the why …

When I awoke.

February 23

GATHERED TOGETHER

There is nothing sweeter
Than family and friends
All gathered together,
Remembering when

We were last together,
Having great fun,
Playing in the leaves,
Or basking in the sun.

Cousins by birth,
Friends by choice;
So many memories,
A reason to rejoice.

We pray for more days
For us to share
The love for each other
That will always be there …

Gathered together.

February 24

GOD-BLESSED

You are God-blessed:
You have eyes to see.
You have ears to hear.
You have been set free.

What a day of rejoicing:
You have feet to walk.
You have a mouth
With which you use to talk.

You have a heart,
A spring in your step.
You have life;
It has meaning and depth.

You are God-blessed,
So be totally aware.
All of these are given to you
By God — we're in His care.

February 25

Build, Spread, Pray

Lord, help us build
Your kingdom in our hearts.
As we meet life's challenges,
From You may we never depart.

Lord, help us spread
Your kingdom to those we meet.
Many are disheartened,
Living lives of defeat.

Lord, help us pray
Your kingdom to come:
Rescuing the perishing
From the evil one.

Coming as a lion,
Cleansing all creation from sin,
History being fulfilled,
From the Beginning to the End!

February 26

Homeward Bound

Traveling can be fun:
Short distances or long, too.
Seeing new scenery,
Discovering new things to do.

Going to your destination one way,
Then coming back a different route,
Admiring the landscapes:
Traveling can be a hoot.

Especially taking a wrong turn,
Going through a quaint little town,
Strolling down memory lane
Before you turn around.

And once again you're traveling;
Now you're homeward bound.
That new scenery was beautiful,
But home is where your heart is found.

February 27

THE CHILL OF MORNING

The cold chill of morning
Gives way to a brand-new day.
What will be in store?
Will it be work or play?

The sun beaming brightly,
Its warmth on your face,
Rejuvenating your spirit
With God's mercy and grace.

A feeling of excitement
Permeates your very soul,
Looking forward to this day
And what it might hold.

As the chill of the morning
Gives way to sunny skies,
The day has truly blossomed
Before your very eyes.

February 28

EXCITED TO BE

Sunday morning we arise,
Have our coffee, realize
How blessed we are today
To be able to offer praise

To the One who brought us through
The night to skies so blue.
And we sit down to read
Our Bible and share, with God, needs …

Not just for us, but others, too.
That's what Jesus says to do.
Ask Him for and always seek
Where He will guide us this week.

We love these Sunday mornings,
The new week dawning.
Just excited to be
Part of God's great family.

February 29

Precious Hope

Precious hope
That in us lies,
Waking up
To our surprise.

Knowing God and
What may be in store,
What He'll give us:
Blessings galore.

Filling our day
With His power,
Seeing us through
Each and every hour.

Precious hope
He instills in all.
We may stumble,
But He won't let us fall.

March 1

Busy, Busy Little Bees

Busy, busy little bees,
Humming around plants and trees,
Pollinating all you touch.
We thank You, Lord, so much

For sending these little ones;
Watching them can be such fun.
But don't get too close to see,
You might get stung by a bee.

The honey some of them make
Is so delightful on a pancake,
Or on a piece of bread
With some peanut butter instead.

God, You created even bees;
Thank you for allowing us to see
The beauty of the simplest thing,
And how much joy a bee can bring.

March 2

Activate My Spirit

Activate my Spirit, Lord;
Let my witness soar
To heights I've never known,
Spreading Your love to more.

To others who are needy,
Or sad, lonely or blue;
Help me share joy
In everything I do.

As I live each day,
Let Your light shine,
And activate my Spirit, Lord,
To show Your love divine.

March 3

The Yard Is Beckoning Me

As I sit here contemplating
On what the day may hold,
The sun is shining on my back.
What task will now unfold?

Should I work in the yard,
Or in my house today?
I think the yard is beckoning
For me to work and play.

The air is brisk and chilly,
Leaves dancing across the ground,
Pine cones scattered everywhere,
And acorns do abound.

The household dirt and dust can wait;
In the yard I want to be,
With that heavenly sunshine
Beaming down on me.

March 4

TOO BUSY!

Sometimes we are too busy
To do the things we should,
To stop and thank the Savior.
How different our day might be if we would

Take the time to meditate
Upon the words we read,
And then put to action
The things we need to heed.

We have just become too busy
In this worldly life we live
To stop and to reflect
On all the blessings God gives.

Lord, when we find ourselves too busy,
Remind us Who is in control;
Help us to stop our busyness,
Your glory to behold.

March 5

Day Has Passed

The quiet night
Closes in;
Day has passed
Once again.

Reflecting back
On my day,
Pure delight,
I would say.

Started out right,
Continued to be
An uplifting one,
You see.

Spent with hubby
And family.
I smile in the quiet night:
What a great day for me!

March 6

AGING GRACEFULLY

I pray I'm aging gracefully;
I pray that others see
All the many blessings
God has given me.

He has shown me mercy,
Filled my life with joy,
Helped my heart to sing
And try to always rejoice.

Days aren't always easy;
Sometimes the body aches.
But I pray I'll always have
A smile upon my face.

Lord, help me age gracefully,
Help my family see
The love of God shining
Always in me.

March 7

A New Week Begins

A new week has begun;
God has put a song in my heart,
Sunshine on my face.
All are just a part

Of a new beginning
To a glorious week;
New adventures to start,
New paths to seek.

Each day is such a blessing,
If we only yield
To God using us,
His love for us to instill

Into each and every hour
Joy should ever abound.
A new week has begun;
Spread happiness wherever you're found.

March 8

Working Together

Working together
Can be such fun:
Accomplishing things
Left undone;

Laughing together
Over silly things,
Bringing a smile;
The heart sings.

Time just flies
When together you work,
Using your hands;
Never, ever shirk

Or put off until tomorrow
Working together today.
Tomorrow may not come,
So don't squander today away.

March 9

THE GRAPE VINE

I see the grape vine budding,
Though green leaves haven't appeared.
I know spring is just ahead;
The birds chirping near.

I feel the warmth of sunshine
As we fertilize the ground.
I see the beauty of a butterfly
As it dances all around.

The earth coming back alive
From winter's dormant state,
And my soul springs with joy
To this season we relate.

As flowers begin to bloom,
Green sprigs of grass appear.
Oh, the wonderful signs of spring,
We welcome you here.

March 10

Watching the Birds

I watched the birds
Fly to and fro,
Gathering up straw
As they go

To build their nest
High in a tree,
So their newborn
Can be

Safe and secure
Way up there,
Free from worry
Or earthly cares.

Until they grow
And flap their wings,
To build their own nest
Come next spring.

March 11

Father, Keep Me Focused

Lord, I choose to follow
Wherever You lead today.
Wherever You take me,
May You shine in me, I pray.

Some of my days are planned,
Some are productive, I see.
Some are just for pleasure,
For rest You give to me.

Whatever my day may bring,
I want to honor You.
I want You to be foremost
In everything I do.

So, Father, keep me focused.
Keep my eyes on things above,
For I am filled with Your Spirit.
Let me shower others with love.

March 12

God, You're Awesome

Flowers blooming everywhere,
Trees budding in full array.
Pollen season has begun;
Looks like a spring day.

Birds are chirping,
Squirrels are scurrying,
March winds blowing,
Green grass growing.

The earth renewed,
Another season has come.
We feel refreshed;
God, You're awesome!

March 13

SUNDAYS ARE THE BEST

A day of worship,
A day of care,
A day of blessings,
For us to share.

A day to rejoice,
A day to sing,
A day to thank God
For so many things.

A day to begin
A brand-new week,
A day to show love
To those we meet.

A day for thankfulness,
A day of rest,
A day of refreshing.
Sundays are just the best!

March 14

Thank You for Mornings

I lie still in the morning;
What are the sounds I hear?
Right now it's very quiet,
Not many noises near.

The night has turned to daybreak;
Not much scurrying thus far.
But it won't be long,
I'll hear the passing of each car.

I ponder just before I rise,
What shall I do today?
There are many places calling:
Should I go, or should I stay?

Come on now, don't be lazy,
The sun beckons to me.
There are times on the calendar,
Places you need to be.

So I'll drink my coffee,
Put on a new face,
Put on my clothes,
Join the human race.

March 14

I'll get motivated quickly
To start my day out right.
There's always lots to do —
On that we can delight.

Thank You, Lord, for mornings
To lie still and hear Your voice,
Then to rise and shine
In a new day to rejoice!

March 15

Winter Is Passing

Trees are budding,
Flowers are in bloom.
Winter is passing;
Lake waters loom,

Beckoning us to come
Enjoy nature's view.
Gifts of God
Created for me and you.

How I love springtime.
The renewal of life begins.
The sun beaming brightly,
The message it sends:

Get up, get busy.
There's work to be done.
Before the day closes,
Make time for some fun.

March 16

Spring Is Near

The roosters are crowing:
Welcome the day!
The sun is shining
In brightest array.

The coffee is brewing,
The smell so divine;
Starting the morning,
What will this day find?

The wind slightly blowing,
The chimes gently ring,
Saluting the day
And all it might bring.

The sights, smells and sounds
I love so dear,
Right here with me;
Spring is near.

March 17

Awake at 4:30 am

Awake at 4:30 am.
What is wrong with me?
I can't seem to sleep;
What is troubling me?

I don't have to worry.
God is always here.
Whatever may come my way,
I don't have to fear.

The moon is shining brightly
Through the window shade.
Oh, the splendor of this world
Our Heavenly Father made.

Now just lie quietly
By your husband's side,
And feel the peace take over
That only God provides.

March 18

FOR ALL YOUR GOODNESS, LORD

Today the earth beckons me
To come work with my hands,
Moving soil from place to place,
One of springtime's demands.

Then to plant and water
And pray for seed to grow,
The beauty of each one
As its harvest begins to show.

Each precious sprout that rises
A miracle of life begins.
It renews our spirits,
Gives deep joy within.

And later as we see the product
Produced by working hard,
We'll bow our heads in thankfulness
For all Your goodness, Lord.

March 19

UP AND AT 'EM

Up and at 'em;
It is time
To get moving.
The clock chimes:

Time for work,
Maybe some play.
Time to get up
And start your day.

The roosters are crowing,
The hens at work,
The goat is bleating,
Your duties don't shirk.

So, up and at 'em;
Get on the stick.
The day is young,
But it rushes by quick.

March 20

I Will Seek to Find

Dawn's early light
Peeks through the blinds,
Bidding me to arise
To explore and find:

What today has in store,
What new avenues to explore,
What this new day will bring,
Will my heart sing?

I bow in prayer
And thank my Father above,
And ask that He
Fill my heart with love.

In dawn's early light,
I will seek to find
My purpose for today,
What the Father has in mind.

March 21

I'VE BEEN GIVEN ANOTHER DAY

The frost shines like diamonds
In the morning sun,
Giving the earth a beauty
As the day has begun.

Spring flowers standing,
Trees blooming all around,
A testament of new life
Everywhere is found.

Cars and buses passing,
Businesses open their doors,
The flurry of people
Wondering what's in store.

Thankfulness flows through me;
I've been given another day.
The wonder of God's glory
In finest array.

March 22

Each Day a Precious Treasure

Another busy day
To do so many things.
A time to share with others
The joy that God brings.

A time for laughter,
For remembering days past.
A time for reflection
On memories that last.

Each day a precious treasure,
A gift from God above,
A time of showing others
How much we truly love.

Love each day of life.
Love each person involved, too.
Love each precious moment
Given by God to me and you!

March 23

Sweet Faces

I see the sweet faces
Worn with old age,
But they are smiling.
You wonder what phase

Of life they are living,
Some minds still strong;
Some not even remembering
Where they once belonged.

But they are so loving,
So thankful to be
Where people can attend to them,
Where others oversee

Their tasks in daily living.
Proud to be a part
Of a loving nursing home staff
That serves them with all their heart.

March 24

Good Night, Midnight!

Almost midnight,
Still awake:
Wondering what
It would take

To make my mind
Go to sleep
So I could rest?
Maybe counting sheep.

There is no fear;
God's within me.
His Holy Spirit
Always here will be.

Guiding me
Through every day,
Helping me,
Showing me the way.

So I'll close my eyes,
Snuggle next to my love.
Sweet dreams, I pray
To God above.

Good night, midnight!

March 25

WAKE UP, WAKE UP

Wake up, wake up.
The day has begun.
What is in store?
A day of fun.

A day to be thankful,
A day to rejoice,
Yet a day of sadness.
Christ made the choice

To be crucified
On Calvary's tree,
A day of atonement
For you and me.

So wake up, wake up.
The victory is won
Through the blood of the Lamb,
God's sacrificial Son!

March 26

Dawn Has Broken

Dawn has broken,
The light shines in;
A busy new day
Now to begin.

Places to go,
People to see,
A time to prepare
For what is to be.

Each day brings
A fresh start
To enjoy the things
Dear to our heart.

So we quickly arise,
Read God's Word, and then
Start the day worshipping
Once again.

March 27

Resurrection Day

The darkness of night,
No moon to shine,
Yet our hearts overflow
With His love divine.

It's Easter morning,
And we recall
The greatest sacrifice
Of all.

We celebrate,
With joy profound.
Jesus is alive,
The sweetest sound!

Resurrection day
We, too, shall face,
Saved by Christ's blood
And His amazing grace.

March 28

STEP OUT IN FAITH

Step out in faith
Never in fear;
The Creator of the Universe
Is always here.

He asks you to trust,
To earnestly obey,
To step out in faith
Each and every day.

Though storms may come,
You should never fear;
The Creator of the Universe
Is always here.

March 29

The Morning After

The morning after
The night before,
So many adventures
To explore.

Will I play outside,
Or will I stay in?
Decisions, decisions;
Where do I begin?

The garden needs sowing,
The beds made and neat,
The beautiful sunshine says to me,
"Get to your feet!"

Come outside and enjoy
The sunshine today.
There's lots to be done,
So get on your way.

Today is fleeting,
Yesterday has passed;
Make up your mind
And do it fast.

March 29

So, on this morning after
The night before,
I'll put on work clothes
And go to explore

Those adventures that await:
Fresh air, sunshine,
Decisions, decisions;
I've made up my mind.

March 30

Step Up to the Plate

"Step up to the plate,"
I hear the Master say.
"There's work to be done
Each passing day."

"The field is white to harvest;
My workers are so few.
Step up to the plate.
Watch what I do through you."

Oh, Father, may I obey
When I hear Your call.
The task may seem overwhelming,
And I feel so small.

Yet You tell me:
"Step up to the plate.
I'll give you the strength.
Go forward … don't hesitate!"

March 31

YOUR ANNIVERSARY

Today is your anniversary;
You've had four years to show
How much you love each other,
How much your love did grow.

My prayer for you is many
More anniversaries to celebrate;
Always let each other know
How much you care before it's too late.

God has joined you together
To share life's ups and downs;
Make your days joyful,
Your love to truly abound.

Happy anniversary, my precious ones.
I pray you'll always know
Marriage vows are sacred.
Continually let your love flow.

April 1

April Fool's Day

April Fool's Day:
A day of fun,
A day to tease
And fool someone.

A day of laughter,
Pulling a prank
On someone gullible,
Thinking you were being frank

And getting to laugh
At your own joke,
And at a friend
Fun to poke.

For laughter is medicine
Straight to the heart.
Happy April Fool's Day.
Now, some fun impart!

April 2

The Earth Replenished

The storm clouds are fleeing,
Beckoning the sun to shine.
The Lord has watered
With His grace divine.

The grass seems greener,
The flowers nourished and fed;
The garden is awakening
Each and every sown bed.

My heart is singing,
What a glorious day;
A time of refreshment
Is on its way.

It was just beautiful,
Even with the lightning and wind,
To see the earth replenished
By God's hand, once again.

April 3

Every Day Should Be Son Day

Every day should be Son Day,
A day to stop and think
Of the marvelous creation
Of earth's and heaven's link;

A day to truly celebrate
Each gift we have been given,
And to use those gifts wisely
In our everyday living.

If only we would realize
The urging of God's plan
And go about our daily lives
Serving God and man.

For every day should be Son Day.
Our hearts should overflow,
For the Master of the Universe
In our lives should always show!

April 4

Take Time to Give God Praise

So far, has been a lazy day,
Yet a day to give God praise
For letting my feet touch the ground,
Knowing His love always abounds.

I'll find the strength I need
To get busy and to heed
The work that needs to be done,
Knowing my strength comes from the Son.

Oh, how precious are the days;
God just always seems to amaze
Me when I really try
His will for me to satisfy.

So on those seemingly lazy days,
Take the time to give God praise.
Then get busy and rejoice;
Listen to the Master's voice.

April 5

Treasured Thoughts

Treasured thoughts
Flood my mind
Of days past,
Those special kinds

That you tuck
Away in your heart,
And pull them out
When apart.

From those loved ones
You hold so dear,
Wishing they
Were living near.

Oh, treasured thoughts
So glad to find,
You're tucked away
In my heart and mind.

April 6

TAKE A WALK

Take a walk
To clear your mind,
To explore the world
And to find

The benefits
A walk can bring —
Especially when
You walk in spring.

Grass seems greener,
Skies are radiant blue.
The sun beaming down,
Warming you.

As you take a walk,
May you always find
Something wondrously new
To occupy your mind.

April 7

So Much in Store

Night has fallen;
Time to settle down.
Look back over today,
And what it brought around.

Started really early
With the sun shining bright.
Ended with cloudiness,
Not a star in sight.

Garden plots filled
With dirt, clay and top soil.
Fertilize tomorrow,
Then we'll start to toil.

Planting and weeding,
Watering and more,
Then harvesting our veggies,
So much in store.

April 8

I Lift Up

I lift up my eyes
To You today,
To thank You, Lord,
For guiding my way.

I lift up my voice
To praise and sing,
For all the joy
To my life You bring.

I lift up my hands
In honor to Thee,
For all the blessings
You have given me.

I lift up my ears
To hear Your voice,
For only through You
Can I truly rejoice.

April 9

Sweet Memories

I look around and see
All the things special to me:
The pictures hung on the walls
And many gifts, large and small.

I see the sweet smiles
On my grandchildren's faces,
And remember the good times
And all the places

We once traveled together —
But those days have passed.
I sit here wishing
They could last.

But wait ... they do —
In my sweet memory's mind:
Those days gone by that
Fill me with joy sublime.

April 10

A KALEIDOSCOPE OF COLORS

The sun shining
Through the trees
Creates quite
A kaleidoscope, you see,

Of mixed colors
To enjoy,
My imagination
To employ.

Dancing around
With beautiful grace,
Making patterns
On the face

Of whatever surface
On which they may land,
Majestically shining
Their display … grand!

April 11

LET THE WEEK UNFOLD

Monday seems to come so fast;
Sunday's day of rest past.
The weekend just flew by,
And we wake up with a sign.

The beginning of a work week
Our busyness will peak,
But by Friday we'll seek
For a day to retreat.

And find somewhere to go,
A different venue to know,
Maybe to take in a show
Or put out new plants to grow.

Whether we are young or old,
Time doesn't stand still, we're told.
Life is precious like purest gold.
Get up, get busy, let the week unfold!

April 12

A Wonderful Day

Almost midnight,
What can I say?
It has truly been
A wonderful day.

Spending time outdoors,
My honey and me,
Then cooking supper
For part of the family.

Going to the gym
With a dear, sweet friend.
What a wonderful way
For my day to end.

So, thank You, dear Father.
I've got blessings galore.
Can't wait for tomorrow
To see what's in store.

April 13

I Am Blessed

I am blessed
Beyond measure.
Christ is
My greatest treasure.

When I arise,
I thank my God
He's placed me on
American sod.

Free to do,
To go, to play.
Free is my soul
Each and every day.

For I am blessed
Beyond measure.
Christ is
My greatest treasure.

April 14

God Is Nigh

As I sit at my table,
Looking out the windowpane,
I see God's handiwork
In each and every frame.

There are green leaves swaying
As He sends a gentle breeze,
And a grape vine blooming,
Pollinated by the bees.

Just one of springtime's pleasures
Sent for us to enjoy,
As we think about the day
And what senses we'll employ.

May we lift our voices in praise
To the One who lives on high.
Take another look outside
And give thanks … God is nigh!

April 15

Friday Friends

We have some special friends
We meet with week after week.
They are the type of friends
Everyone should seek.

We laugh and play together,
Eat together on Friday night,
Enjoy each other's company;
Sharing with them is a delight.

We all have grandchildren.
Ours are "grown-er" … some of theirs, babes.
We show pictures and brag,
And sometimes even rave

About their accomplishments
Just like grandparents should do,
Telling how much we love them,
Our pride showing through.

So far, we're the only ones with great-grands,
So we get to brag a little more,
Telling them how great it is
And what they'll have in store.

April 15

We love our Fridays together
As our friendships continue to grow.
We know we can count on them;
They always say, "Let us know."

If you need a helping hand
Any day or any night,
You know you can call on them;
They'll help make your burden light.

We thank You, God, for our "Friday friends,"
Seven days of every week.
They are truly the kindest folks
You could ever meet.

April 16

A Walk Through the Woods

Nothing like
A walk through the woods
To get motivated
For the things you should …

Appreciate each moment
Of every single day,
The beauty of God's creation
In perfect display.

Trees stand majestic,
Wild flowers at their feet;
Birds singing loudly
As they dig for a treat.

No, there is nothing like
A walk through the woods
To get you motivated
And realize God is so good!

April 17

TIME SLIPS BY

Time has a way
Of slipping by.
It's the top of the morning,
Then nightfall is nigh.

So much to do,
So many places to see;
Yet time slips by,
Except for eternity.

So be ready, pilgrim.
This world is not home.
One day we'll travel
To a place we've never known.

But, oh, the joy
When we reach that destiny;
If we received Jesus,
We'll be alive … eternally!

April 18

Playing in Dirt

Today we worked
Out in the dirt,
Our faces brown,
Our feet a mess,
Dirt in places you'd never guess.
If you had seen us
You'd surely say,
"They played in dirt today."
Playing in dirt
Was so much fun
When we were young ones.
However, working in dirt
Brings on aches and pains,
But, oh, the beauty it brings
When the flowers bloom in spring.

April 19

Our Day Begins

Our day begins
With quiet time
To reflect on God's Word,
Hearing His voice divine

Speak to us
In various ways,
Telling us what to do
On certain days.

Are we to visit?
Or call a friend?
Or work outside
Until day's end?

Whatever the task
Before us today,
We won't begin
Until we pray!

April 20

Death Came Knocking

Death came knocking
Once again today.
An angel came,
Swept my aunt away

To her true home.
She's been looking for so long
To see many loved ones
And hear heaven's song,

Where she'll never grow older,
Never shed a tear.
She was so ready
To leave here,

Joining her loved ones,
Never more to depart.
Her final wish granted
That she held deep in her heart.

April 21

UP BEFORE DAWN

Up before dawn,
The sun yet to rise.
Wash our faces
And the sleep from our eyes.

Sip on hot coffee,
Read God's Word, then
Get ready for the day.
Where shall we begin?

So much to do,
Many places to go.
We've got to get busy
If we want our garden to grow.

As the sun rises,
Our strength is renewed.
Thankful for another day
God's given me and you.

April 22

Days Fly By

As I get older,
The days fly by.
Looking for an adventure,
I begin to sigh.

Where will I go today?
What will I do?
Who will I see?
Will it be something new?

I am just so thankful
To have another day
To explore my options
And be able to say:

Thank you, God, for the years
You have given me;
I am truly blessed
As days fly by, you see.

April 23

FRIENDS

Lord, I'm so thankful
For so many friends.
I'm grateful for the love
That never ends.

None of us are perfect,
But we all know
We'll stick together
And our friendship grow.

We'll tell each other secrets,
We'll share memories galore.
Even when we're not together,
We'll never ignore

That we are friends
And forever will be.
Thank You, dear Father,
For giving so many friends to me.

April 24

G-RATED LIFE, X-RATED WORLD

We truly live in an X-rated world,
A world where sin is always hurled.
A world where perverseness is the norm,
Where evilness is no longer mourned.

Surrounded by sin every day,
Christians are called away.
They are called to live a life
Full of worldly troubles and strife.

Let the world know you detest sin,
That you hate it and won't enter in.
But let your light shine
For Jesus Christ … all the time!

Let your identity always be
That "Christ is alive in me,"
A sinner saved by God's grace,
Letting others know who took our place.

Do not associate with those practicing sin,
But pray and attempt their souls to win.
As the Holy Spirit deals with them,
Making sure their religion isn't just a whim.

April 24

Like hermits we are not to live,
But to these sinners always give
Hope for a future with the Lord.
Show to them it's not that hard

To discern right from wrong.
God can make you very strong,
Let you test the world's ways,
And realize sin doesn't pay.

But sin is unpleasing to God above.
Help them realize God is love.
They can be freed by amazing grace
If only they will seek God's face.

Living in this X-rated world
Where Satan's darts are always hurled,
Stand up for Jesus day-by-day.
He is the truth, the life, the way!

April 25

YOU ARE WONDERFUL, LORD

The sun is shining,
The birds singing, too.
Oh, how wonderful, Lord,
Are You!

Being able to rise,
See the beauty all around.
Your greatness, God,
Truly abounds.

Help me today
To show love.
Wherever You lead,
I'll look above.

And say thanks
For all You do.
Oh, precious Lord,
How wonderful are You!

April 26

Family Remembrances

Spending time with family
Is so much fun,
Remembering the "good ole days,"
All the things we've done.

Cousins together laughing
About good times and bad,
Days when joy abounded,
Even some that were sad.

Growing old together
Though we may be miles apart,
Still always thinking
About each other in our hearts.

Then when reuniting,
Those days are so sweet.
Reminiscing about the past
Makes our lives complete.

Lord, as long as we're able,
Let us get together when we can
To laugh until the tears flow,
Remembering once again

April 26

Those childhood days we shared,
The crazy things we'd do.
We are so thankful, Father,
We owe our lives to You!

April 27

Traveling

Traveling can be
So much fun,
Clear blue skies
And glistening sun.

Music playing,
You sing along.
Or lift your voice,
Sing your own song.

Watch other travelers
As they go by;
Some of them
Seem to fly.

Life can be
So much fun,
Traveling around
With your loved one.

April 28

True Joy

True joy is seeing
Your grandson's first home,
Him showing you with pride
How much he has grown.

Since you first held him,
And he stole your heart,
The love you've shared
That will never depart.

The pride he's brought you,
The accomplishments he's achieved,
It truly pays off
For a grandmother on her knees,

Praying for his safety,
For him and his bride.
This precious grandson
You know God will guide

To where he belongs,
Singing and playing his guitar,
Making beautiful music, too.
True joy, Seth, you are!

April 29

A Child's Hug

A child's hug
Means trust and love, too,
A caring gesture
From them to you.

Their sweet smiles,
Their tender skin,
Their cheek touching yours.
You become their friend.

Help us, like children,
To always be
Loving and caring,
Like them, to see

A child's hug
Goes a long, long way
To fill us with joy
Each and every day.

April 30

CELEBRATING

Celebrations are so much fun,
People gathering around,
Laughing, talking, hugging,
Joy seems to abound.

Whether it's a birthday
Or a holiday event,
Just being together
And realizing what is meant

By sharing with each other
Special times in our lives,
Times of wonderful memories
That later are realized

To be such happy moments
That pass so quickly by.
Celebrating together …
That's where true joy lies!

May 1

Joy in the Morning

Joy in the morning,
When we rise to another day.
God has brought us through the night
In His own special way.

The sun peeks through the curtains;
Its warm glow fills us anew.
A new day is beginning;
What's in store for me and you?

The smell of coffee beckoning,
Get up on your feet,
Explore the world around you;
Aromas, oh, so sweet!

Joy in the morning,
Another day has begun.
Thank You, Heavenly Father,
For being our Living One!

May 2

STORMY DAYS

Stormy days are here,
Lightning flashing across the sky,
A kaleidoscope of colors
And thunder from on high.

The earth seems to rumble,
Trembling and afraid.
"Stay away from windows,"
Mother used to say.

We'd all huddle together,
Feeling safe and warm;
Together we would weather
Even the fiercest storm …

On stormy days.

May 3

The Strawberry Patch

Today I picked
From the strawberry patch;
Washed some up
For a breakfast snack.

Red and delicious,
Each and every bite;
Full of nutrition,
What a delight!

Grown in our garden,
Fertilized, watered each day.
Picked when they're ripened
In April and May.

We truly enjoy
Our strawberry patch.
Each sweetened by God,
His glory … unlatched!

May 4

Just Sit and Chat

Our lives get so busy.
We don't take time to chat,
To sit out on a porch
And chew the fat

The way we used to do
Way, way back when
We were very young.
And it seemed then

We made time for neighbors,
Weren't always on the go.
Truly took the time
Our neighbors to know.

How did our lives get so busy
We can't just sit and chat?
I'd like to see us get back
To where we could chew the fat!

May 5

Sunset

Sunset is beautiful
As it fills the western sky,
So many varied colors
Pleasing to the eye.

The darkness fast approaches;
Daytime is spent.
The beauty of the sunset,
A spectacular event.

Sometimes I truly wish
The sunset had no end,
But then I think:
When would a new day begin?

May 6

Making New Friends

Today was a day
To make new friends.
Wherever we go,
The Father always sends

Someone to welcome
Into our lives.
Just like us,
They really strive

To live life fully,
To spread true joy,
To give an uplift
And to employ

All the love
We receive each day.
We love making new friends
Along our way.

May 7

Family Fun

Today was filled
With family fun:
Eating lunch,
Then getting to run

Around the town
From store to store,
Making memories,
Then going some more.

A birthday party,
Children all around,
In and out the door,
Their joy abounds.

I think we'll sleep
Very good tonight.
Family fun,
What a delight!

May 8

MOTHER'S DAY

Mother's Day,
A special time.
Families gathering,
Love sublime.

A day to honor
Our mothers dear,
Whether they're far away
Or living near.

Presents and flowers,
Calls and cards, too.
Things held dear
By Mother, from you.

So celebrate Mother.
Always let her know
You appreciate her;
Let your love for her show.

May 9

Our Solid Ground

When life gets hard,
No need to despair.
God is with you;
He knows your cares.

When you need strength,
He'll make you strong.
Go to Him;
He's always along.

For He never leaves;
He never forsakes.
Trust in Him.
He's the One who takes

Struggles and strife
And turns them around.
He's the Rock of Ages.
He's our Solid Ground.

May 10

In Your Heart, Keep a Song

Lord, give me grace
Today, I pray,
To touch some life
That comes my way.

Help me to be
A friend to all,
To lend an ear
When someone calls.

I want to live
My life with zest,
Attempt to do
My very best.

For time is short,
Though it may seem long.
Do yourself a favor:
In your heart, keep a song.

May 11

LIFE IS SWEET

There's a garden to hoe
And grass to mow,
Flowers to water, too.
There's always lots to do.

But life is sweet,
And the yards look neat.
Though we become tired,
Our handiwork we admire.

It won't be but a week,
And once again weeds will peek.
So we'll hoe and mow
And watch our gardens grow …

For life is sweet!

May 12

A DAY AT THE LAKE

A day at the lake:
Sitting on the dock,
Not having to worry
About watching a clock.

An ideal setting
For a day to reflect
On happy times
And to respect

God for all His
Blessings given so free.
A special time at the lake
Will always be

A precious memory
For me to look back on.
A day at the lake,
Then back safely home.

May 13

CELEBRATE LIFE

Celebrate life
So others can see
Just how precious
Life can be.

For if you live
Life at your best,
Others will see you
And they will attest

To your faith,
To your trust, too,
In the mighty God
Who looks over you,

Helps you celebrate
Each and every day
The life you're given
On this earthly highway.

May 14

Favorite Fishing Hole

A perfect day
To grab a pole
And spend some time
At a favorite fishing hole.

Bait your hook
And soon you'll see
If there's a fish
Just waiting for you or me.

The sun beams down,
A warm breeze blows,
A smile on faces,
True happiness glows.

For today we went
To a favorite fishing hole
To renew our bodies
And refresh our souls.

May 15

WAKE UP, IT'S SUNDAY

Wake up, it's Sunday morning.
A new week has begun.
Time to make new memories,
One by one by one.

The sun is shining brightly;
Look out your front door.
Grab a cup of coffee,
Sit down and explore.

See what God has to say
In your daily Bible reading today.
Then get up, get dressed,
Off to church. What a great way

To start off a new week
With all your Christian friends.
So many blessings are in store
Before this new week ends.

May 16

RISE AND SHINE

Rise and shine.
I hear the rooster crow:
Get out of that bed;
There's work to do, you know.

We chickens need some feed;
The old goat does, too.
The garden needs tending;
So much for you to do.

Don't waste a minute.
Time does not stand still.
The older you get,
You realize this statement is real.

So, rise and shine;
This day is fresh and new.
There is no telling
What God has in store for you!

May 17

Rain

Rain has fallen
Most all the day.
But our joy
Is here to stay.

For just a moment
The sun broke through,
Refreshing our spirits,
Alive and renewed.

The flowers elated,
The gardens, too,
For the refreshing rain,
Knowing what it will do

To strengthen them,
To allow them to grow;
God showing His power.
Lord, thank You so …

For rain!

May 18

Our Temporary Home

A cool breeze blowing,
An overcast sky.
A very pleasant day,
No one can deny.

The green grass of spring,
Flowers in various colors abloom,
Picked at their peak,
Fragrancing any room.

Birds singing sweetly,
Their memories abound,
Building their nests
Where their young ones are found.

Until they can fly
Out on their own,
They'll live like us
In their temporary home.

May 19

Turtle Rescue

Today there was a turtle
Trying to cross the road.
It was moving slowly,
Trying to find a new abode.

Afraid it might be hit
By a car passing by,
Hubby and I decided
We didn't want it to die.

We performed a turtle rescue;
Took it back where it belonged:
Down on the creek bank,
Where it could find a log.

The turtle seemed happy,
And we were, too.
The rescue of a turtle
Instead of making turtle stew.

May 20

Early Morning Phone Calls

An early morning phone call
From a granddaughter so dear
Makes our day joyful,
Makes her seem very near.

Our grandchildren are scattered,
Some near, some far away.
We earnestly pray for them
Each and every day.

We pray for their happiness,
Their health and wealth, too;
For the joy of God's love
We instilled in each of you.

So these early morning phone calls
Are precious to us, you see.
It makes our hearts soar
To know you're thinking of Papa and me.

May 21

Sunset

As the day fades,
The sunset arrives;
Its endless beauty
Fills the skies.

Wherever you are
At this time of day,
You truly wish
The sunset could stay.

But, oh, so quickly
It rushes out of sight,
And in its place
Comes the darkened night.

May 22

Happy Fifth Birthday, Isaiah

Five years ago, God gave us
A precious "little man."
What joy filled our hearts
As we held your tiny hands.

Oh, how your mother loved you;
How proud today she'd be
To see her baby boy
Turn five years old, you see.

I know she's saying "Happy birthday!"
From heaven up above,
And sending hugs and kisses
And all of her love!

Happy fifth birthday, Isaiah!

(This was written for my first great-grandson to honor him and his mom, Lisa Marie Bledsoe, who went to heaven on October 5, 2011.)

May 23

In Your Time

In Your time
All things come to pass,
The seasons of our lives,
Until at last

Earthly life is over,
Our new life has begun.
We have fought the fight,
Our earthly battle won.

Help us to look forward
With excitement day by day,
For it's in Your time
We'll all be swept away.

Some to heaven's glory,
Some to hell's torment.
Just make sure you are ready
For this last earthly event.

Repent!

May 24

ANOTHER SEASON

Spring is almost over.
Another season will begin.
The days pass so quickly,
And summer is here, my friend.

Graduations, parties, the beach;
There's so much more.
Days of celebrating summer,
Places to go galore.

But before we know it,
Fall will come our way.
We'll look forward to coolness
As summer slips away.

Then the winter comes.
We want to see some snow.
Then before our eyes,
Another season "springs" again, you know.

May 25

LIVE LARGE

Each day of my life,
I want to live large.
I never want idleness,
To me, to be charged.

I want to grow spiritually;
I want to share
The love of my Father,
Showing others I care.

I want to be kind,
Gentle and sweet
To all the people
I have the privilege to meet.

Living large is important;
Life here passes so fast.
I want to leave a legacy
To my family that will last.

May 26

It's All a Gift

When we think of talents,
So often we forget
The One who gave them all.
Yet, face-to-face we haven't met.

For all we have is given;
We don't gain it on our own.
Sometimes it's hard to realize
Until we have spiritually grown.

Realizing the Creator
Of the earth and skies and seas
Is the greatest of all givers,
For He created you and me.

Thank Him for your gifts;
Use them wisely and see
It's all a wonderful gift
God has bestowed ... free!

May 27

Friend Friday

On Friday evenings,
You know where we'll be:
Spending time with friends,
Having fun, you see.

Catching up on the news,
Sharing pictures and more;
Eating a meal together,
So many memories to store.

We truly look forward
To Friend Friday each week.
Going to places together.
Life is sweet!

May 28

Remembering Grandma

It is raining,
With the sun shining bright.
You know old folks say,
"The devil is beating his wife, all right."

So many little idioms
I heard my grandma say
Are coming true
Day by day.

"Little children step on your toes;
Big ones step on your heart."
I didn't understand way back then,
But now I'm living that part.

I love remembering Grandma,
Her smile and tender embrace.
I pray my grandchildren will cherish
The smiles they put on my face.

May 29

Find Victory

It is through the darkness
We find the Light.
When our world seems upside down,
Hope seems out of sight.

It is at this moment,
We begin to realize
We can't go it alone;
We need God on our side.

So, don't despair, dear one.
Put your trust in God and see
The darkness will be dispelled,
And you'll find victory!

May 30

Memorial Day

Memorial Day:
A time to reflect
On all the ones
We need to show respect

For giving us freedom
Through all the wars past,
And providing our safety,
Our gratitude forever lasts.

How blessed we have been
To be born in the land of the free.
What a marvelous gift
God has given you and me.

So truly celebrate today
And give honor where it's due.
Salute all those who serve
The Red, White and Blue!

May 31

In the Early Morning Hours

In the early morning hours,
When all is quiet and still,
You lie next to your love
And wonder: Is this real?

The peacefulness you feel,
The look upon their face,
That look of true contentment
That cannot be erased.

You think, I am so blessed
To have you by my side.
What did I do to deserve
This one to whom I confide

My hopes and my dreams,
My deepest thoughts and prayers;
In the early morning hours,
I'm thanking God you are there.

June 1

Lightning

The sky is filled
With thunderheads,
Streaks of lightning,
Yellows and reds.

Thunder rolls;
Rain is yet to come.
We sit and watch
In the comfort of home.

Though lightning is beautiful,
It can be deadly, too.
God showing His power
To me and you.

Safely inside,
I'll enjoy the show
And afterwards look
For a beautiful rainbow.

June 2

Goodies from the Garden

It's that time of year
When gardens grow
With all types of veggies
We all enjoy so.

Being able to harvest,
And then clean and cook
Those delicious veggies,
And then the next day, look

For more of the goodies
That we freeze or can.
Then when winter comes,
We'll have on hand

Goodies from the garden
We picked in springtime,
To enjoy all year long.
Yummy … sublime!

June 3

BUSY DAYS

I thank God
For busy days.
Working hard,
Then getting to play

"Hand and Foot"
With our best friends.
What a great day
With a perfect end.

I thank God
For giving us a chance
To enjoy life
As we advance

Far into the golden years,
Staying busy still.
Being blessed day by day,
Living life with zeal!

June 4

Family Reunion

Today was a family reunion:
Uncles, cousins and friends,
Smiles, hugs and kisses
Given without end.

Tales of fun times,
Some true, some stretched a touch;
Laughter and giggles,
Things that mean so much.

There was joy on everyone's faces;
Picture taking, delicious food, too.
Seeing old, old pictures,
Hearing about our heritage anew.

How I love a family reunion,
And all the love it brings.
May we keep them coming;
They're one of life's most precious things.

June 5

Soft, Gentle Rain

There's a soft, gentle rain
Falling all around.
It came so quickly
Without making a sound.

It's the kind of rain
In which I love to play,
Bringing sweet memories
Of past yesterdays.

It gently caresses
Each blade of green grass, too,
And kisses the flowers,
Refreshing them anew.

Then silently,
It slips away.
This soft, gentle rain
That came today.

June 6

Thank You for the Rainbow

The colors of the rainbow
Flow in front of my eyes.
Each one very special,
I've come to realize

The majesty of creation
Of the God Who loves us so,
Who gave His Only Son
So that I might know

How very, very precious
Is this life given to me,
And what an awesome God
Who has given me victory.

Each time I see a rainbow
Appear up in the sky,
I'll bow my head and say
Thank you to my Father on high!

June 7

"I Am" Can

The sun shining on the wind chime,
Glimmering like a bright star
From the dew of the morning,
Beckoning from afar.

Arise and explore;
There's so much to see.
A whole world of adventure
Waiting for you and me.

Oh, how I love the morning
After a lengthy day of rain,
With the colors of the rainbow
Dancing on the windowpane.

My heart bursts with pride
When I see the Master's hand,
And He reminds me once again,
"I am! I am! I can!"

June 8

LET FEAR FLY

Let fear fly;
God has a plan.
Fears rob the soul
And causes man

To shrink in despair
And really miss out
On God's perfect plan
Because of doubt.

God's perfect love
Casts out all fear,
Fills us with blessings
Year after year.

So, let fear fly.
Make it go away.
The Master of the Universe
Is in control every day!

June 9

SEEK GOD

When the morning arrives,
Seek God to know
What He has planned,
Where you are to go.

Throughout your day,
Seek God to see
His mighty power
Alive in you and me.

When the night falls,
Seek God and rest.
His timing is perfect;
He always does what's best.

When we seek God
At the beginning of each day,
He'll bring the joy
If we seek His way!

June 10

GOD DID IT AGAIN!

Today as we were traveling,
I thought of God's wondrous grace.
I thought of His tender mercies
And the love I'm allowed to embrace.

I thought how often He's brought me
Through very trying times,
And sheltered me from harm
With His arms divine.

I thought of all the blessings
On me He has bestowed,
And of all the heavy burdens
When He carried my load

Upon the Cross of Calvary,
Washing my sins away,
And how He brought me safely home.
God did it again … today!

June 11

A Great Day

Today was a great day,
Gathering with old friends.
The very kind of day
You hate to see end.

Reminiscing about old times,
Sharing pictures galore,
Having a scrumptious luncheon,
Then reminiscing some more.

Times like these are treasured,
Buried deep within.
Hoping that in one year
We can do it all again.

June 12

Sunset, Sunrise

Day is coming
To a close,
Sunset shining
Like a beautiful rose.

So many colors
On display,
A wondrous climax
To our day.

Time to rest,
To go to sleep,
Praying to the Lord
Our souls to keep.

Tomorrow will be
A new sunrise.
What will the day hold?
Maybe a great surprise!

June 13

The Clouds

The clouds tell a story.
Just look up to see
What your imagination
Thinks a cloud may be.

I see a fish;
You see a clown;
I see an elephant;
Just look around.

All kinds of formations.
Let your mind soar.
Look for something special
You've never seen before.

God made the sky
For us to enjoy.
So look up at the clouds,
Its beauty employ!

June 14

SUMMER IS AHEAD

Summer isn't even here,
But, boy, the days are hot!
You go outside to work awhile,
Then come inside to plop!

The heat will drain you;
You must rest awhile.
Your mind says it's okay,
But your body is in denial.

We all must be careful
Not to get outside and scorch,
Because if we don't,
We'll look like we've been torched.

So be careful, summer is ahead.
We all must be wise;
Let our bodies tell us when
It's time to come inside!

June 15

Each Day Is So Important

Each day is so important,
So grab it by the horns.
It may be filled with joy,
Yet, it could be forlorn.

What is so important
Is to do the best you can,
To make each day count
And lend a helping hand

To your mate, family, or neighbor,
Or a stranger along the way,
Using your God-given talents
To make someone else's day.

So wake up with enthusiasm,
Let each day begin
Filled with vim and vigor,
Being thankful without end!

June 16

JUST WAIT

Playing the waiting game
Is hard to do.
There is so much
Waiting for you:

A house to clean,
A floor to sweep,
A garden to hoe,
An appointment to keep.

However, sometimes waiting
Can help, you see.
What you had planned
Wasn't meant to be.

So just be patient;
Take waiting in stride.
Lay down your frustration
As you decide …

To just wait!

June 17

A Busy Day Looms

A busy day looms,
So much to do ahead.
Better get an early start,
Jump quickly out of bed.

So many days for us are planned,
Others just seem to flow.
Whatever might be the demands,
We will always know

God the Father is in control,
Will guide our every step,
Even on those busiest days
When we really feel inept.

So rise with lips of praise,
A song in our heart.
Though a busy day looms ahead,
Thank God and get an early start!

June 18

THE DAY BEFORE FATHER'S DAY

The clouds are lingering in the sky,
Yet the sun peeks out to say:
"Arise and start your day."

The birds flying to and fro,
Squirrels scuttering around so,
It's a blessed day, you know.

Saturday has come to end the week;
We look forward and seek
On Father's Day to speak

Words of love that we recall,
When we were very small
And our daddies seemed so tall.

Encouraging us to be strong.
Stay away from all wrongs.
That our heart to Jesus belongs.

To wish Him and our dads
Happy Father's Day!

June 19

The Clouds God Created

The sun is shining brightly,
Giving the clouds a special glow.
A vast array of colors
Putting on quite a show.

It appears God has taken
A paintbrush in His hands,
And created little wispy clouds
That change on His command.

Some are soft and fluffy,
Others thin and rushing by.
All of them are beautiful
As they float across the sky.

Oh, how blessed we are
When we have eyes to see
The clouds God created
And displayed for you and me.

June 20

A Day to Reminisce

Today was a day to reminisce
About days gone by and feeling blessed,
To know that we have come so far
From yesterday to where we are.

So many years under the bridge,
A life to live, a heritage.
What will others remember one day
When all of this has passed away?

Will others remember our face?
Or recall some special place,
Where we laughed and prayed
And felt the joy of those yesterdays?

Reminiscing … good for the soul,
Especially when you've grown old.
You will get there someday, my friend,
If you are blessed enough your old age to ascend!

June 21

A Peaceful Heart

A peaceful heart,
Dear Lord, I pray,
Give this one
Each and every day.

Banish my fears,
Help me to see
There is no need,
For You live in me.

May I never feel
Overwhelmed by circumstance,
But stare it in the face,
Realize it's a chance

For my true colors
To really shine,
Like a peaceful heart
With an uncluttered mind.

June 22

IN OUR COUNTRY HOME

Darkness sets in,
Nightfall has come;
Safe and secure
In our country home.

Listening to music,
Watching TV,
No better place
On earth to be.

How blessed we feel
To live in this place,
Slightly hidden from view
With lots of space

To enjoy the darkness,
The quietness of night.
In our country home,
Snuggled up tight.

June 23

Strawberry Moon

Strawberry moon,
Shining so bright.
What a glorious glow
You're giving off tonight.

How large you loom
So high in the sky.
Not quite full,
Yet we're not denied

Your wondrous beauty
That lights our way,
Replacing our sun
That's gone for the day.

How blessed we are
To be able to see
God's marvelous creation
On display for you and me.

June 24

THE STILLNESS OF MORNING

In the stillness of the morning
Before my day has begun,
I thank my Heavenly Father
For all the things He has done.

The rest time of the night,
My body to renew.
As the sun rises,
I see the glistening dew.

A new day for adventure;
What will be in store?
Excitement on the horizon,
New things to explore.

In the stillness of the morning,
My spirits start to soar.
Arise, get up quickly.
See the beauty just beyond the door.

June 25

WHERE WE BELONG

I love to walk to the garden
To see what has grown overnight,
To gather the vegetables and fruit
We eat with such delight.

Our hearts swell with thankfulness
For the bounty grown by our hands,
For being able to work diligently
To harvest from our land.

We are blessed beyond measure.
No hunger in our home.
So many delicious meals.
Who could have ever known?

That in our longevity
We could still be strong,
And plant a luscious garden
Right here where we belong.

June 26

Too Hot

The thermometer says 100 degrees;
I think I'll stay inside.
I surely don't want to bake
Or have my skin fried.

Wishing I had a pool,
Then I could get cool fast.
But at my age,
I guess that's too much to ask.

So, I'll just chill under air-conditioning,
Make it a lazy day.
Since it is truly too hot
To go outside and play!

June 27

Traveling Mercy

Lord, today I'm praying
For traveling mercy divine;
I know that you are in control,
So please take care of mine.

The roads pose so much danger;
There's drugs and drinking galore.
So I'm asking for traveling mercy
From the Savior I adore.

These are my children,
My grandchildren, too.
I ask for Your guidance
For You to see them through.

Their travels may be lengthy
Or just down to the store.
I'm still asking for traveling mercy
Just like I've done before.

Thank You, Father.

June 28

Some Days

Some days start out as planned;
Others seem to go astray.
That's when you go back to bed
And say, "I'll start over today!"

But each day should be filled with joy;
We don't know what tomorrow will hold.
So we need to be prepared
For whatever might unfold.

Our days are precious,
Whether great or few.
So when a bad day starts,
We need to take a review.

See why things went awry,
What we could do to change the day.
Start all over and display
Thankfulness to God and pray!

June 29

SPECIAL DAY

Today's a special day
For my daughter and son-in-law.
They've been married 25 years,
I know they look back in awe …

Saying, "How did we make it
Through all those ups and downs?"
But they endured the trials,
That's where true love abounds.

On this special day,
I salute them.
They never gave up
On the slightest whim.

May God continue to bless and
To their marriage vows stay true.
I want you to know, my darlings,
I'm so very proud of you.

June 30

Enjoying Home

There are times
I love to wander,
But it seems now
My heart's grown fonder

Of being in my home,
Sitting and looking around
At all the treasures
That abound.

Pictures of my children,
Grandchildren and great-grands, too.
Thinking of the fun times
And things we used to do.

Now that I've grown older,
My favorite place to be
Is enjoying home
With my hubby next to me.

July 1

July

The first day of July
Came so very fast.
Seems like spring just came,
But it sure didn't last!

The temperature is soaring,
The sun hot and bright.
Outside can be miserable,
Except late at night.

But there is a reason
For each season of the year —
And before we know it,
Christmas will be here.

We'll relish the month of July,
Even with unbearable heat.
We know fall is coming quickly
With cooler weather … what a treat!

July 2

Let My Life Be Fragrant

Lord, let my life be fragrant,
Giving off an aroma sweet.
So others living about me
May know joy and not defeat.

For if my life is fragrant,
Others will want to know
How I was able to attain it.
So Christ to them I'll show

By telling them of Jesus,
The One who set me free
By dying on a cruel cross
That day at Calvary.

May my fragrance permeate
Every life I meet,
So they can carry this sweet aroma
I found at Jesus' feet!

July 3

FAMILY TIME

Family time is so important:
Getting together, sharing days,
Remember all the fun
We've had along the way.

Laughing and talking,
Sharing old stores when
We'd sit around the table,
Get up and then

Scatter around the house,
Taking a nap or sharing a chore.
Oh, what precious memories
We all have to store.

Always make time for family;
They won't always be around.
But when they're gone, you'll recall
Where true love was always found.

July 4

Independence Day

Independence Day:
A special time of the year
To thank all the people
Who sacrificed far and near

Giving a salute
To the Red, White and Blue;
Pledging our allegiance
To the nation we hold true.

Honoring our forefathers
As independence they declared,
And remembering the sacrifices
They were called to bear.

Let freedom ring forever
In our blessed USA,
As we truly celebrate
And give thanks for Independence Day!

July 5

GRANDCHILDREN

It's wonderful to have grandchildren
Who have grown up to be
Faithful, kind and loving
To "older folks" like me.

They listen to our stories,
(Share and remember, too)
Of days gone past,
The things we used to do.

And we love hearing the tales
Of adventures they've made anew,
As they explore new territories
Freshly charted with you.

Their visits seem so short,
But the memories are here to stay.
We cherish them in our hearts
Until they visit again one day!

July 6

The Rain

Outside, the rain pours down,
Watering the earth below.
It came here so quickly
Before it had to go.

It left behind puddles
That are soaking up so fast.
I really hoped it would stay awhile
To rejuvenate our grass.

Our garden now looks perky,
The stalks standing tall.
Full of delicious vegetables
To delight us all.

The temperature dropped fifteen degrees;
Steam rose from the asphalt highways.
It sure was nice to have the rain.
Thank You, God … we sure needed it today!

July 7

Isaiah's Smile

The sweet little boy
Smiling at me
Is named Isaiah,
And I'm privileged to be

His guardian for the day,
Watching him as he plays,
Hearing his precious voice say,
"I love you more, GiGi" today.

The image of his mother
In heaven above,
Her same disposition,
He is such a love.

I don't have to go
Too many miles
To see this wonderful child.
Oh, how I love Isaiah's smile.

July 8

Bumps in the Road

There are bumps in the road
Along life's highway.
We often succumb to them
Day after day.

Some pertain to our health,
Others to our soul,
Some to our minds,
All trying to take control.

We must fight the battles,
Whether great or small.
Standing strong and firm,
Refusing to fall.

Sometimes bumps are good;
They keep us on our toes,
Help us to remember
God sees, hears and knows.

So take the bumps with grace.
Let them be a learning tool.
Remember life is precious,
Live by the "Golden Rule."

July 9

I Am Unique

I am unique,
Made in the image of God.
Given life and breath
To live upon earth's sod.

An instrument of the Father
To spread His holy Word.
Given strength and power,
Praying others heard

The message of salvation,
Given to tell each day
To those sent in our path
Along life's busy highway.

Let my light shine,
Let Christ be seen in me
To help win the lost
That they might live eternally.

July 10

Going Through Storms

There are many storms
That come into our lives:
Strife, and many struggles,
Sometimes in disguise.

Our health may start to fail,
Our minds grow dim and weak,
Our spirits seem so low;
It's then we begin to seek

Release from these storms.
On whom will we call?
Where will we fix our eyes
As we begin to fall?

Where will power come from
To overcome these trials deep?
Who can we plug into
When these tribulations creep

And catch us unaware,
Unprepared for what has come?
Help us to remember
Where our help comes from.

July 10

Father, as these storms rage,
Help us to hear Your voice:
"You're never alone, My child.
Now, dear one … rejoice!"

July 11

HOPELESS

When things seem hopeless
To Jesus, go.
He can instill hope;
He can let you know

He constantly abides
Wherever you are.
He works for your best;
He truly cares.

Don't let discouragement
Seep in to stay.
Give it to God.
He'll take away

That hopeless feeling,
Put joy in your heart.
Our Master divine
Will never depart.

July 12

THE SHEPHERD

The Shepherd feeds me.
I'll never hunger again,
Whether it's for food
Or physical demands.

The Shepherd leads me.
I'll never go astray,
But if I should,
He'll show me the way.

For my Shepherd tends to me,
Body, mind and soul.
He'll draw me back
Into His fold.

The Shepherd guards me
Throughout the day and night,
For the Shepherd loves me.
In Him I delight!

July 13

Running Ahead of God

Have you ever found yourself
Running ahead of God?
Thinking it's okay,
God will spare the rod?

God wasn't acting fast enough,
So we just run ahead,
Knowing all the while, where we're going
He hasn't led.

Very soon we realize
We were so very wrong
To run ahead of the Father.
We weren't where we belonged.

Lord, thank You for Your mercy
When we run ahead of You,
For turning us around,
Allowing us to do what You intended us to!

July 14

LIFE'S STREAM

Standing on a bridge
Above a mountain stream,
Watching the water rushing,
So peaceful and serene.

I think of my life.
Which direction did it flow?
What pathways or obstacles
Helped to make me grow?

I think of childhood days,
Of playing in nearby streams,
Hearing the water moving
As I stood there and dreamed.

Then later, when my children
Would swim in a nearby creek,
Hearing their shrills of laughter
As the waters tickled their feet.

The years passed so quickly,
Just like the water in the streams,
And they became adults
With their own hopes and dreams.

July 14

So I stand here reminiscing
By this West Virginia mountain stream,
Watching the water rushing
So peaceful and serene.

July 15

Coming Home

Leaving for a trip
Is so much fun,
But coming home
When your week is done …

Tired and weary,
Yet refreshed, too.
Thinking of all
The things you must do.

Getting back to the routine
With all the daily chores,
Until once again
You can travel some more.

I truly love traveling,
But I can say:
Coming home is wonderful,
In your own bed to lay.

July 16

Saturday Morning

I enjoy Saturday morning
Lying a little longer in bed,
Thinking about my day
And what may lie ahead.

Thanking God for my blessings,
All my family and friends.
Planning my day
From beginning to end.

Then the phone rings.
Who could it be?
Someone wanting to chat
Or checking on me?

Whatever the day holds,
I'm just happy to know
God gave me another Saturday morning
To love, live and grow.

July 17

STRESSES OF LIFE

Stresses of life
Can weigh you down,
But there is a place
Where relief can be found:

Down on your knees,
Talking with God,
Giving Him your burdens,
Leaning on His rod

That is steadfast,
Always secure.
His listening ear
Helps us endure

The stresses of life
That weigh us down,
And puts us back
On solid ground.

July 18

WAITING

Sitting and waiting
Isn't my forte.
I like answers;
I want them today!

But waiting is necessary
In some cases, you see,
For things to develop.
So we may as well be

Content with waiting,
Like time standing still.
We can't rush the Lord;
Just pray for His will!

July 19

DAYS

Some days seem endless,
Like they'll never end.
Some days seem short
Before they even begin.

But each day is precious,
A gift to use.
Use it wisely, my friend,
Never, ever abuse.

For life at its longest
Is fragile and sweet.
Give it your best;
Never give in to defeat.

Whether the day seems endless
Or too short to you,
Enjoy it with pleasure,
Whatever you do!

July 20

Wake Up Anticipating

Wake up anticipating
What the day may bring:
Showers of true blessings
Making my heart sing.

A call from a friend,
Or a visit from someone dear.
Maybe a little excursion,
Blue skies, the weather clear.

However the day unfolds,
I'll bow my head and say
With vibrant anticipation,
"I'm looking forward to today!"

July 21

Difficult Times

Sometimes our lives are made up
Of very difficult times,
When we begin to wonder
Is this ever going to end?

What did I do to deserve this?
What is wrong with me?
Things were running so smoothly;
What could the problem be?

Maybe all the struggles
Are to make me realize
God is growing my character.
Why am I so surprised?

We're not promised life will be easy.
A beautiful rose has thorns, you see.
But, oh, the precious aroma we smell,
God's gift to you and me!

July 22

Family Reunion

It's time for a family reunion.
Relatives far and near
All coming together,
Sharing moments so dear.

Some we see yearly;
Some once in a while.
Hugs and kisses galore
And beautiful smiles

To say, "I'm glad to see you,
So happy you could come."
Some you're even wondering,
"Where did they come from?"

I love our family reunions,
The food, family and fun.
I'm really looking forward
To being here for another one!

July 23

Traveling Home

Packing up to travel
Back home once again.
Two days seem so short
To be with family and friends.

The joy we feel being together
Is truly worth it all.
Reminiscing, making new memories
Till home calls.

We decide to travel a new route,
Unexplored territory to see.
How beautiful this earth
God made for you and me.

Though we may be tired and weary,
Our home is a haven of rest.
So we travel with anticipation
To get back to our own little nest.

July 24

The Deadly Sin

Allowing anger to rule our lives
Brings on trouble and strife, friend;
Causes us sorrow and pain.
To us there is no gain, no end.

But God says, "Wait, My dear friend,
Don't let anger sneak in."
That's where we go wrong:
Letting murder begin.

Not controlling our emotions,
Letting anger flow free;
Not being able to look ahead
To what it's doing to you and me.

There are consequences;
They affect God and man.
A division of humans
In our great land.

People become divided,
Distanced from God, too.
But there is a cure
Waiting for me and you:

July 24

Make amends quickly;
With humility, bow down.
Admit your part of the anger.
Let forgiveness abound.

So, don't allow anger to seep in
To rule your days, my friend.
Be humble yourself ... forgive.
Keep away from this deadly sin!

(Read Matthew 5:21-26)

July 25

Hen, Get Back In!

I looked out the window,
And what to my surprise?
One of our hens
Was wandering around outside.

She wouldn't let me catch her,
So we scurried to and fro.
She's a pretty smart chick.
Back in that fence she didn't want to go!

But I was persistent;
She wasn't going to get away.
So up and down that fence we ran,
Persuading her to stay.

Finally, I got her cornered,
Opened the gate real wide.
She looked up at me
And pranced herself inside!

July 26

In His World

In the world,
Not of the world,
Is who I want to be.

A Christian influence
In the world
So others might see

The Heavenly Father,
The grace He gives
Abundant and free.

And when I die,
I want to be
In His world, eternally!

July 27

LIVING IN PEACE

I have a body,
A mind and a soul.
I have a spirit
That lives … I'm whole.

Made in God's image,
Like Him, to be
Holy, set apart
To live eternally.

I am not perfect,
But I should strive
To be like Jesus,
In Him abide.

Living in peace
At all times in every way,
The Lord God with us
Day after day after day.

July 28

You're In or Out

Lord, it seems these days
You're either in or out.
You're following the world;
You're deep in doubt.

You feel the world tugging
In your life day by day.
You don't want to yield;
You know that's not God's way.

God says, "I won't forsake you.
Be courageous and strong.
Delve into My Word;
It'll keep you from wrong."

"Meditate on My promises.
I've not broken one yet.
Never fear or be dismayed.
I have paid your debt."

Oh, Father, count us in;
Keep the world out.
We have Your assurance;
We no longer have to doubt!

July 29

GRANDDAUGHTER FUN

Our youngest granddaughter
Is so much fun,
Whether taking her to a movie
Or playing in the sun.

Watching a movie
Or something on TV,
Sitting beside her
Fills my heart with glee.

Saying nighttime prayers,
Watching her as she sleeps,
Joy just overwhelms me
As I sit and rub her feet.

Granddaughter fun
Passes way too fast,
So you'd better enjoy it.
Those sweet memories will last.

July 30

A Day at the Beach

A day at the beach:
Sand, sea and sun,
Waves rolling in,
We jump each one.

Sea shells crushing
Beneath my feet,
Sand castles built
In the summer heat.

Kites flying high,
Beach balls and more,
The sea gulls flying
Up and down the shore.

A day at the beach:
Peaceful and serene,
All kinds of people
Here can be seen.

July 31

A Storm Is Brewing

A storm is brewing,
Dark clouds in the sky.
Thunder is rumbling,
Lightning nearby.

We need the rain.
Everything is so dry.
It will be a blessing
From heaven on high.

A respecter of storms
I've always been.
I'll stay inside
When the storm begins

And thank our dear Father
For the wind and rain
That nourishes the earth,
All life to sustain.

August 1

Run-Down Shack

I went to visit
At a run-down shack today,
But the love I felt
No one could take away.

A daughter living with her mother,
Giving her such tender care.
No luxuries to surround her,
Sitting on the porch in a wooden chair.

A roof over their heads,
Fans blowing around hot air,
Cracks in the floors and ceiling,
Cupboards almost bare.

But there was something very special,
No complaints, no sign of despair.
In this little run-down shack,
I felt love everywhere.

August 2

THE BEGINNING AND THE END

One minute there is sunshine;
The next, darkness looms.
How will the day unfold?
True happiness, or gloom?

It is said your destiny
Is how you treat the day.
Will you say, "Come on, sunshine"
Or "darkness, come to stay"?

Friend, you should know by now
You are not in control.
The Master of the Universe
Is the One who holds

Each moment and each hour,
Whether darkness or sunshine to send.
So thank Him in all circumstances;
He is the Beginning and the End!

August 3

LIFE IS LIKE A QUILT

Life is like a quilt:
Each stitch sewn with love,
Putting hours of time into it
With patience from above.

Pieces sewn together,
Just like the years of life.
Memories to unfold,
Some good, some full of strife.

The finished product beautiful
To last for many years,
Given to someone special
Who to you is very dear.

You pray they will enjoy it,
And remember you each day
As it is displayed proudly
Where it may lay.

August 4

NOW A MAN

Our little baby boy,
Born twenty-eight years ago,
Is now a grown man
With so many talents to show.

The memories I hold dear,
So very deep in my heart,
Began when he came into the world
And immediately became a part

Of my life every day,
Helped me through times of despair,
Has given me so much love;
Lets me know how much he cares

About his grandmother who
Has adored him from the start.
My baby, now a man,
Still holds the keys to my heart!

August 5

BUSY DAYS

The best days of all
Are when we begin
By waking up early
To help a friend.

Go to the doctor
Or the grocery store,
Go out to eat,
Or shop some more.

Laughing and talking
Is so much fun.
A busy day ended
With a dear one.

The best days of all
Are when they end,
Until the next time you're called
To help a special friend.

August 6

HAPPY BIRTHDAY, JESSICA

Today is Jessica's birthday.
We want her to know
We're so glad she's family;
We hope it always shows

How proud we are to have her
As our granddaughter-in-law so dear.
We pray she'll have many more
Birthdays for many more years.

We love you, sweet Jessica.
Hope your day is as special as you.
You are our grandson's proof
Dreams really do come true.

Celebrate your day
With those you love the most.
Make it one to remember.
To you we raise a toast!

August 7

A Time to Worship

I love my Sundays:
A time to worship and sing,
A time of joyful reunion
With my church family it brings.

A great way to start the week,
Renewed, rejuvenated, refreshed.
A special time of togetherness,
Then an afternoon of rest.

Later, it's back to church:
A Bible study to enjoy,
Studying with fellow Christians,
Afterwards, fellowship we employ.

When back at home we settle down,
A deep peace in our hearts,
We find the time to worship
Before a new day starts.

August 8

SITTING ON THE DECK

I'm sitting on the deck,
Watching clouds roll in.
I can smell the rain,
Wondering when it will begin.

The flowers and garden are begging,
"Rain, come and stay awhile."
Seems I can audibly hear them;
I begin to smile.

As the rain hears their plea,
I feel a drop or two;
Then it begins to pour.
I say, "God is hearing you."

I sit for just a moment,
Then get up and go inside.
Grab me an umbrella,
"Thank You, Lord," I cried!

August 9

School Days

It's that time of year again:
School is about to start.
Teachers and students meeting,
Shopping at Walmart.

Homework and study hall,
Report cards and so much more.
Exciting times for all involved,
Looking forward to what's in store.

How I remember those days
So long, long ago.
Every day was a challenge,
Always wanting to know

What I would do
When school days would end.
If all I've learned since,
I'd been aware of then!

August 10

Exercising

Exercising: good for the soul,
Good for the body, I'm told.
Gives your mind a workout, too,
Especially as you grow old.

Exercising makes you strong,
Improves your stamina, it's true.
So exercising — keep it up.
It really is good for you.

Some days it seems like fun;
Other days, you wonder why
You punish yourself so
But continue, and sigh.

Psych yourself up to exercise again,
Remember the benefits at the end.
Exercising: good for the body, mind and soul,
Keeps you from getting old.

August 11

Don't Fret About Tomorrow

One day the stresses
Of life will be gone.
We'll be at eternal rest
In our heavenly home.

No more sorrow or tears,
No more death or pain.
If we love God and are His,
Death will be gain.

To live with this promise
Gives us peace in our souls,
Gives us assurance of salvation
Whether young or old.

So don't fret about tomorrow;
Live life fully each day.
The reward is out of this world,
And the time is not far away.

August 12

Starting Off the Morning

Starting off the morning
With Bible study and prayer
Makes the day go smoother,
For God is always there.

Pushing us to go forward,
To share with others around
The precious love of the Savior,
Where true love is found.

Allowing us to be witnesses
Of His tender care,
Giving life great meaning
Anytime or anywhere.

So always start your morning
With God's Word and prayer,
Making your day go smoother,
Whatever you may have to bear!

August 13

Meteor Showers

Last night, the meteors flew
Across the northern sky.
A beautiful array of stars
Seen with the naked eye.

A breeze blowing gently
To whisk the heat away,
And make the perfect ending
To a blessed summer day.

God's handiwork manifested
In the beautiful sky above,
A true testimony
Of His undying love.

I truly enjoy the meteor showers
With my daughter by my side,
As we watch the heavens together,
My precious Traci and I.

August 14

Relaxing Time

The sun is shining brightly,
The temperature soaring high;
But we are cool and cozy,
Tucked away inside.

Papa is taking a nap
While I watch TV,
Relaxing until it's time
For church again, you see.

These quiet Sunday afternoons
Quickly come and go.
You learn to appreciate them,
Those days that pass by slow.

Life just gets so busy.
It's nice to have a day
When we can spend time
Whittling the hours away.

August 15

Each Day a Perfect Canvas

Mondays seem so busy,
So very much to do,
Getting an early start
To see what is new

On this week's agenda,
The days to explore;
So much to experience,
Wondering what's in store.

Each day a perfect canvas,
A work of art to paint.
Living life with thankfulness,
Not letting the world taint

Even one precious moment
Of every day that begins
From dawn's wondrous light
To sunset's marvelous end.

August 16

Full Moon

Full moon shining so bright,
In the western sky you loom,
Casting beautiful shadows
All across the room.

The grass seems to glisten
From the glorious light,
As a gentle breeze blows,
Cooling down the night.

It's said full moons cause mischief,
But I truly wonder why,
Because it shines so brightly
From high up in the sky.

Tonight, I'll wish upon a star,
As I look at the heavens above,
And thank my God for creating the full moon
And showering me with love.

August 17

Fellowship

There is nothing like fellowship
With our dearest friends,
Sitting around a table
As the day ends.

Sharing all our stories
Or jokes we've heard today;
The perfect time to listen
Before we go our separate ways.

Hoping it won't be long
Before we meet again,
Sitting around a table
Fellowshipping once again.

August 18

Kiss Sadness Goodbye

Tonight, I'm feeling very sad;
I really don't know why.
I think back over the years
And wonder why they had to fly.

But time does not stand still;
We wouldn't want it to.
We wouldn't want to miss out
On doing the things we do.

Like raising our children,
Then seeing them all grown up.
Being very proud parents,
Our hearts seem to erupt

When we see our grandchildren,
Our great-grandchildren, too.
Just thinking of them makes me smile
And chases away my blues.

Though I was feeling sad,
Reminiscing about old times
Makes my heart feel lighter,
Knowing life is sublime.

August 18

And so when I feel sad,
I'll just ask myself, "Why?
You've had a wonderful life."
Kiss sadness goodbye!

August 19

Dinosaur in the Sky

Today I saw a dinosaur
In the clouds above so high.
From its mouth came lightning
Streaking across the sky.

It was quite a show,
Exciting, I must say,
As I wondered what other creature
I might see today.

I thought of God's creation,
Of all the things He made,
How each one is magnificent.
His marvels never fade.

My love for clouds will continue,
No matter how old I get.
I might just see another dinosaur
Breathing lightning yet!

August 20

HEATHER

Twenty-eight years ago,
Our precious Heather was born.
The years have flown by quickly
Since God did adorn

Our lives with a precious granddaughter,
Our very first, you see.
How very lovely she has grown,
Makes our hearts swell with glee.

I wish for her great blessings,
Happiness, health, a life complete.
For she deserves the very best;
Her smile is, oh, so sweet.

Happy birthday, dear Heather,
May God grant you many more.
We are looking forward
To what else God has in store!

August 21

FRIENDS

Oh, how I love my friends.
Each and every one;
Each of them unique,
All of them such fun.

Whether we're at church
Or at a restaurant to eat,
Our fellowship together
Really can't be beat.

Sometimes we may play cards
Or just sit and chat awhile.
Talking about our families
Always makes me smile.

I pray all my friends
Enjoy my company, too.
I love them each and every one
The way You taught me to do!

August 22

Working Out

Working out
Can be such fun
When you walk beside
A loved one.

You get to talk
Or watch TV,
Listen to music
And sometimes see

A friend or acquaintance
You haven't seen for a while.
You get caught up;
There are hugs and smiles.

So, working out
Is not drudgery to me.
It's something I enjoy
Especially with my daughter by me!

August 23

Awakening with Excitement

When I awoke this morning,
I realized during the night
That God was orchestrating
What I would do in daylight.

I woke with excitement,
Hardly could contain myself.
I knew He would be with me
Whenever my bed I left.

I don't know what He's planned;
I just know I must go
And be about His business
As I try to show

His love to all I contact
Or witness to each day,
For He has great plans for me
If I follow His way!

August 24

God Uses Laymen

God uses laymen
In His work each day,
Just ordinary people
Leading the way

To Jesus Christ our Savior
Through common things they do.
Sharing life together,
His love in them shows through.

A willing vessel to go
To do the work at hand,
Laymen who are obedient
To the Father's command.

Taking God's Word with them,
Witnessing along life's way,
Giving your testimony,
Any time, any day!

August 25

Collecting Roosters

I love collecting roosters,
Small, large or miniature-size.
I love their many colors,
So pleasant to the eyes.

So many to me were given
By very special friends.
They hold wonderful memories
That will never end.

I've even got a quilt
Made with loving hands
By a special lady.
Lots of roosters … it is grand!

I love roosters so much;
We have them on our farm.
I love hearing them cock-a-doodle-do;
They are our morning alarm.

August 26

WHERE HOPE IS FOUND

The darkness engulfs us,
Blackness all around.
You see a distant light;
That's where hope is found.

You follow the light
That seems so far away,
And realize before too long
It's the break of day.

And hope bursts forward;
You're given new life, you see.
The darkness is dispelled,
Blackness has to flee

Until the night unfolds,
Darkness comes back around.
You see a distant light;
That's where hope is found.

August 27

A Friend's Birthday

We celebrated a friend's birthday,
And it was such fun.
We all surprised her,
This precious one.

The shock on her face
Was such a delight.
As we all sang,
It was quite a sight!

So many friends and family
Sharing in her special day.
It means so much to be a part
Of celebrating this way.

I pray for many birthdays,
Filled with joy galore,
To celebrate with those you love.
Who could ask for more?

August 28

Thankful Days

This is one of those thankful days:
A day to lift hands in holy praise
To thank our Heavenly Father,
Our voices to Him raise.
This is one of those thankful days.

This is one of those thankful days:
A time to reflect on the week past,
On what we did or what we said.
Will it a shadow cast
On one of those thankful days?

This is one of those thankful days,
For another week has begun.
What will it have in store?
What victories will be won
On one of these thankful days?

August 29

Prayer Is a Privilege

Prayer is a privilege
Our God gave
For us to communicate,
A road to pave

To thank our Father
In heaven above
For bestowing on us
His magnificent love.

A time to praise
His hallowed name,
To thank Him for His kingdom
Where we will one day reign

Along with Him
And those who've gone before.
We can't even imagine
What He has in store!

August 30

Early Morning Quiet

In the quietness of early morning,
I arise and I am blessed.
I look around my home;
I thank God for my rest.

The sun peeks through the blinds
As a new day begins to unfold.
I look over at my husband
And I truly behold

The wonder of our love;
How gracious God has been
To give us twenty-five-plus years.
I pray He will extend

Many more early mornings together,
For us to cherish until when
He calls each of us home.
What a great life ours has been!

August 31

Dog Days

These are "dog days,"
I truly believe;
You can't walk outside
Without gnats that seize

Every part of your body,
Especially your face.
You slap and fan,
But they're in every place.

You hurry inside,
And you pray,
"Lord, just help us
Get through these 'dog days.'"

September 1

A Special Day

Today was a special day,
Meeting and making new friends.
Realizing we had so much in common,
A friendship to flourish without end.

It's amazing when you meet strangers,
You all love the same things.
The more you talk with each other,
You realize the joy each one brings

To make our lives much richer,
Knowing none of us will forget
The happiness we all felt
In those first moments when we met.

I look forward to special days,
Meeting and making new friends.
What a wonderful feeling;
You can hardly wait to see them again!

September 2

Storm Blowing In

A violent storm
Is blowing in;
Lots of rain,
High, high winds.

Pine straw blowing,
Flowers bowing down;
Leaves and trees
Falling to the ground.

Chickens hustling
To get in their pen,
Safe from the storm
They're sheltered within.

Lights are blinking,
Some power lines down;
We're safely inside.
Lord, Your grace abounds!

September 3

Sunny Saturday

Today is a sunny Saturday
After a turbulent storm.
Things are calm and peaceful
On our little farm.

We are so very grateful
For the Father's care;
We didn't know what to expect.
We didn't even dare

Go out into the storm
Until it had passed by,
And we began to see
A beautiful, clearing sky.

We're so blessed this sunny Saturday
That our home and farm were spared
From what could have been.
Father, Your mercy was truly shared!

September 4

Family Times

Today was such a special day,
Family here to celebrate
The birthday of our granddaughter.
Being together was great!

I love these family times:
Eating, laughing, sitting around,
Enjoying each other's company;
That's where true love is found.

The merging of families,
Making memories to share.
Such special moments,
Showing how much we care

That we are connected,
Even if we live miles apart.
Always thinking of each other,
Always in each other's hearts!

September 5

MY BABY BOY

I sit here, reminiscing
About my baby boy.
How much love I have,
How he has brought me joy.

I think of how happy I was
When the nurse first handed him to me.
This firstborn child of mine
That will soon turn fifty, you see.

I wonder where the years went;
They passed by so fast.
From tiny baby to adult,
It's really been a blast.

His health is really failing.
I want him to always know
I love him more than I can say;
I hope it always shows.

September 6

God's Grace

God's grace is sufficient
To see us through each day.
Whatever the situation,
He's the only way

To calm our deepest fears,
Make our worries fly.
For He's the One who sustains us;
He hears our every cry.

Whether it's an illness,
Or traveling mercy we need,
We can always call on Him;
We know that He will heed

And answer every prayer,
If it's in His will.
Maybe not the way we wanted,
But He will answer still!

September 7

A Day in the Kitchen

A day in the kitchen,
Canning is such fun,
Knowing in the winter
We'll be the ones

Enjoying the goodies
We canned today.
They'll taste so fresh
When it's cold and skies gray.

If you've never tried it,
I encourage you to
Spend a day in the kitchen,
Seeing what you can do!

September 8

THE DAILY GRIND

We all wake up
To the daily grind,
Discovering what chores
We will find

To keep us busy
Throughout our day;
It sure won't be boring,
I've learned to say.

Something old or new to do:
The daily grind, it's true,
Takes a lot of inner strength
From me and you.

But we start it out
With a true daily grind:
Our cup of coffee
To wake up our mind!

September 9

SEASONS OF BEAUTY

One season passes,
Another slips in.
The beauty of each
Will never end.

The summer green,
With a vast array
Of beautiful flowers
To enjoy each day.

Then fall arrives;
Its splendor abounds,
As turning leaves
Fall to the ground.

These seasons of beauty
Throughout the year
Are like our lives,
Full of joyful tears.

September 10

The Morning Air

The morning air,
With a touch of chill,
Is so inviting,
Gives your body a thrill.

Thinking of cooler days
And brilliant skies,
As the summer passes
Before our eyes.

A renewed spirit
From deep within.
Thanking the Master
Who always sends

The morning air,
A cup of coffee in hand,
A wonderful day
At His command!

September 11

911 Emergency Call

911 Emergency Call:
On our knees we fall
Before our God of grace,
Prostrate on our face.

In times of trouble,
We all begin to muddle.
Precious Lord, take my hand.
I just don't understand

Why this is happening to me.
Father, why should this be?
Make Your presence known,
Lord, You hear me groan.

Is there a lesson to learn?
My heart within me yearns
To realize what this is about.
Father, why do I doubt?

I know life is short.
Your holiness I exhort.
Humankind is impotent.
Before You we need to repent.

September 11

Depravity in our hearts,
Deceitfulness is a part
Of our everyday lives.
When will we arise?

Become committed to the Cross.
This world is lost,
People living for self
Even unto death.

Lord, we need nobility around,
A people serving others to abound,
Reacting to the world's needs.
Lord, help us to heed.

An opportunity for evangelism awaits,
Giving our all before it's too late.
Praying earnestly day by day,
Father, show us the way.

911 Emergency Call:
On our knees, let us fall!

September 12

Rain, Rain, Come Our Way

Rain, rain, please come our way.
It's so hot; the ground so dry.
Pour out Your blessings
From Your wonderful sky.

The clouds are darkening, we see.
Rain, please come our way.
The plants and grass are begging.
Please come, we pray!

The thunder begins to rumble,
Lightning streaks across the sky.
The rain begins to fall;
We let out a sigh.

You've heard our pleas,
Blessed us once again.
Thank You, Heavenly Father.
Your lovingkindness never ends!

September 13

A Storm May Be Brewing

The darkness engulfs us.
The moon attempts to shine.
The stillness of the night;
Could this be a sign

A storm may be brewing,
Heading our way?
What will we find
When the darkness gives way to day?

We pray for protection
To keep us through the night,
So when we awaken,
We'll see the sun rise bright.

September 14

The '64 Girls

I love meeting
With the '64 girls;
So much laughter
There is unfurled.

Talking of old times,
Of school days when
We were unsure
Where we would end

Up after graduation day.
What we would do?
Would we be scattered?
Would our friendships stay true?

For the '64 girls
Who meet once a month,
My wonderful "blood" sisters,
A God-loving bunch!

Let's have lunch!

September 15

COTTON-CANDY CLOUDS

Cotton-candy clouds
Dominate the sky,
So white and fluffy
As they hurry by.

The sun so bright,
High up above,
Warming our spirits with
A touch of God's love.

Butterflies fluttering,
Their colors so grand,
As they go from plant to plant
Upon our farm land.

Those cotton-candy clouds
Turning to gray
As the sun goes down
On this lovely day.

September 16

DAY TRIPS

Today we went exploring
With two of our kids.
We took a day trip
To see if we could rid

Ourselves of daily chores,
Just wander and have fun.
Just the four of us
On the run.

Did a little shopping,
Then, of course, out to eat.
Seafood was our menu;
It was quite a treat.

Oh, how I love these day trips,
A few hours to unwind
And spend time with family,
Leaving worries behind.

September 17

LATE-NIGHT DATE AT THE GYM

Tonight was one of those nights
We had a late date at the gym:
Me working on the treadmill,
Full of vigor and vim;

My sweetheart waiting patiently,
Talking with people nearby
While I was exercising.
Got to firm up those thighs.

My favorite thing of all
Is to lie in the hydro-bed,
Getting a quick massage
While clearing up my head.

I enjoy our late-night dates,
Even if it is just to the gym
While my husband waits patiently.
I'm so in love with him!

September 18

Arise to Shine

Wake up, sleepy head,
Arise to shine.
It is Sunday morning;
You need to get to church on time.

Get the coffee brewing,
Your Bible close at hand.
Start your day with Jesus,
He always understands

Whatever you are thinking,
Where your priorities lie.
He's forever interceding
From His throne on high.

So get up and get going.
Don't let a second waste.
There is much to do,
So do it with haste.

September 19

FALL IS ALMOST HERE

Just outside the window,
The sky is bright and clear.
A slight crispness in the air;
Fall is almost here.

Leaves are turning colors,
Some falling to the ground.
You see the signs of fall;
You just have to look around.

Collards and turnips planted,
Pumpkins begin to grow.
All the signs we see,
Helping us to know

Cooler weather is coming.
We usher it in with cheers,
Hats, gloves and jackets,
One of our favorite times of the year.

September 20

God, Bless Our Farm

God, bless our farm,
Each acre of this ground.
It is such a blessing,
Just look around

Our house, our garden, our animals,
All part of Your plan.
We dedicate it all to You;
We realize it's by Your hand

We are able to enjoy
These remaining years of life.
Living on this wonderful farm,
It's our earthly paradise.

So continue to bless our farm;
Keep us healthy, we pray,
So we can take care of the things
You give us day by day.

September 21

Beginning Till End

There's so much
I want to do,
Places to travel,
Acquaintances to renew.

Life at its longest
Seems so short.
I want to live
Each and every part

As if tomorrow
Might never be,
Filled with joy
For all to see

How thankful I am,
How blessed I have been
From my life's beginning
Until its end.

September 22

WHATEVER GOD CHOOSES

The sky is gray this morning;
I'm praying for some rain.
It's been several days,
But I shouldn't complain.

These last few days have been cooler;
There's been a lovely breeze.
Leaves are now falling;
Soon there'll be barren trees.

It's that time of year,
Colors galore begin to abound.
Red, greens, yellows, and gold
Begin to cover the ground.

I won't let the gray skies
Make me sad or blue.
There's always a silver lining
In whatever God chooses to do!

September 23

I Am So Blessed

I am so blessed
I woke up today.
I've got a roof over my head;
I am free to pray.

I have food to eat,
Clothes on my back.
There is nothing
I truly lack.

I know I am loved.
I love others, too.
I am so blessed;
What about you?

September 24

Forever Dear

Today was a day
Of sweet memories,
Times I cherish
And hold so dear.

Friends made many,
Many years ago;
Some live close,
Some live not so near.

But it seems like
Only yesterday
We worked together,
Side by side.

Our love only grows
Deeper each year.
These friends I cherish
To me will be forever dear!

September 25

CHRISTIAN FELLOWSHIP

There's nothing in this world
Like Christian fellowship:
Eating, laughing, talking,
Not giving a flip

About what time it is,
Or going home to watch TV.
We're enjoying each other;
Such wonderful company.

I know God is smiling,
Saying, "This is how it should be.
My loved ones together
Is precious to me."

Thank You, Father, for Christian friends,
For companionship and more.
One of God's greatest blessings;
To You we give praises galore!

September 26

Visiting Friends

Today we went to visit
Some dear and special friends.
They, too, live in the country
On a road that's a dead-end.

Their garden is full of goodies
They share so frequently.
Makes my mouth water;
Fills my heart with glee.

We just sat and chatted,
Talked about our family.
Shared some stories,
Sat on the porch to see

If deer would come around,
So many on their place.
We so much enjoyed
Visiting friends … God's grace!

September 27

It's Midnight

It's midnight.
Darkness closes in.
Stars shining bright.
Distant lightning begins.

Shadows in the moonlight
Give an eerie chill;
The earth's stillness
Seems surreal.

Sleep wants to come,
Yet, it evades.
Eyes begin to close,
Trying to persuade

Your body that it's midnight,
Time for you to rest.
Sweet dreams await.
You are blessed.

September 28

A Winding Road

Today we traveled
On a winding road.
What would lie ahead
Would be a heavy load.

For one we loved dearly
Had truly gone home.
No more a clouded mind,
No more will he roam.

For in God's timing,
This loved one was healed.
Yet, our grief and sorrow
Is so very real.

But one day we'll travel
To where he has gone.
Reunited, forever,
Never again to be alone.

September 29

IN THE QUIETNESS

In the quietness of the morning,
Surrounded by God's grace,
In the beauty of this land,
I behold God's face.

Everywhere I look,
His glory truly shines.
The trees, the birds,
All a spectacular sign

Of the Master being here,
Soothing the troubled soul,
Bringing peace in the hearts.
His wondrous love unfolds.

So, in the quietness of the morning,
My mind is at peace.
The God of the Universe
Bids my sorrows to cease.

September 30

LAID TO REST

Today a precious man
Was laid to rest,
His body returned to the ground;
A hard scene, I confess.

But yet a celebration,
Knowing someday we'd be
Reunited in our spirit,
Receiving true victory.

For life is like a vapor;
It disappears so fast.
So many who've gone before
We'll see again at last

On that day of resurrection
When God's chosen will arise,
Be caught up in a moment,
Carried up into the skies,
Laid to rest
Where no one dies!

October 1

You Have Kept the Faith

Christian life is a fight,
One that we can win.
Whatever may come our way,
We can overcome sin.

The Father is in heaven,
The Son interceding day by day,
The Holy Spirit guiding us
In God's wondrous way.

The race is a hard one,
The road rocky and steep.
But the love of the Savior
Runs true and deep.

When our earthly journey is over
And we arrive at heaven's gate,
May the Father say, "Well done.
You have kept the faith."

October 2

The Everest of Ethics

God gives us laws
By which we live.
The "Golden Rule"
To us He gives.

This is the Everest
To which we should climb.
His Word to us
Is so divine.

Treating others respectfully
Is a positive thing,
A positive precept
To which we should cling.

The law and the prophets
On this rule abounds;
Kindness to others
Is where it is found.

The persistent pursuit of God,
Obeying His Word,
Help us keep His commandments
Knowing we've truly heard

October 2

What the Father says
We should do,
In loving others —
Even those who

Don't treat us fairly,
Who cause us pain.
If we treat them fairly,
We will gain

A crown of righteousness
At our journey's end,
When the Father says,
"My child, come in."

October 3

BLESS THIS HOME

Bless this home,
Dear Lord, I pray.
Keep all evilness
Far, far away.

Let Your Spirit dwell
Within these walls,
That visitors know
You are our all in all.

Our home is truly
Treasured ground;
Built on You,
It's firm and sound.

Fill our lives
With things that are good.
It all comes from You,
This we've always understood.

Bless this home!

October 4

Decorating for Fall

Today I decorated
My home for fall:
Pumpkins and turkeys,
Some large, some small.

Such beautiful colors
Warm my heart.
Oranges, greens and browns,
Maroons and yellows are part

Of the hues of the season
That will abound,
Until winter breaks forth
And they're no longer around.

Oh, how I love this
Wonderful time of the year,
Decorating for fall
I'll always hold dear.

October 5

FIVE YEARS HAVE PASSED

Five years have passed
Since you said goodbye.
From this earthly home
To the one in the sky.

But you are remembered;
You are found in our hearts.
Though we can't see you,
You are still a part

Of all who loved you,
And love you still.
For in our minds, sometimes
It doesn't seem real

That God took you away
At such an early age.
Though five years have passed,
Sometimes it seems like yesterday.

October 6

Girls' Night

Being together is fun,
For a girls' night, you see
With those you love,
Watching a movie or TV.

Eating unhealthy snacks,
Laughing out loud, too,
Reminiscing of old times
While making some new

Times to remember
Until together again,
I truly pray
We'll have girls' night, when

We can have more fun,
Make more memories to share.
Just me and the girls,
Any time, anywhere!

October 7

SAFE JOURNEYS

Lord, we pray for safe journeys.
We pray for those left behind.
We pray for grace and mercy.
Protect our bodies, souls and minds.

We know when we travel
Our safety is in Your hands.
Help us to always be aware
Of obstacles and understand

Your enduring love is guiding us,
Keeping us safe from harm.
Help us to be alert and patient,
Not to be alarmed.

You alone provide safe journeys
Whether near or far away.
Someday we'll take our final one,
Safe with You forever to stay.

October 8

Listening to the Storm

We lie awake for hours,
Listening to the storm,
The winds gusting wildly,
But we're safe within our home.

We hear the rain beating
On the roof and windowpanes,
And pray a prayer of protection
As its intensity gains.

It suddenly becomes silent,
But we are aware
It will only be for a moment;
It's still raging somewhere.

And just as it left briefly,
It came back with a fiercer roar.
And we lie listening to the storm,
Safely tucked inside once more.

October 9

Is There Hope?

Is there hope
For this world today?
We have failed God;
We have gone astray.

But God is in control,
Even when life is hard.
He never leaves us;
He is always on guard.

God always leaves a remnant
When the world turns upside down.
We've read it time and again
How He turns things around.

God tells us if His people
Will humble themselves and pray
And seek His face,
He will hear them every day.

But they must turn
From their wicked ways of sin,
So that He might dwell
Deep in the hearts of men.

October 9

Lord, rooted and grounded in love,
May we always stand.
For in You there is hope
For even the vilest of human man.

October 10

God Moving

Do you see God moving
In the world today?
Do you know His kingdom
Will never go away?

The harvest is ripe,
But the laborers are few.
The harvest is plentiful,
Waiting for me and you.

God is moving.
We need to be moving, too.
God is pleading.
What will you do?

October 11

A Day to Sleep In

Today was a day
I needed to sleep in,
Because of a restless night
From beginning to end.

Thoughts crowded my mind
As I lay awake,
Praying for situations
That really need a break.

Talking to my Father
Who hears my every plea,
Knowing He will answer
Because He already sees.

I truly needed a day
To just sleep in,
And listen to His voice
And the sweet release He sends.

October 12

A Walk to the Creek

Today I enjoyed
A walk to the creek,
Talking with my daughter
As we would seek

To gather cans
Along our way
To turn in
For a little pay.

It was so much fun
Just to breathe clean air.
Side by side,
Being able to share.

Just mother and daughter
On a walk to the creek.
Sweet, sweet memories
In my heart to keep.

October 13

A Granddaughter Day

Today is going to be
A granddaughter day.
She's spending the night
So we can play.

We walk outside,
Feel the sun on our face,
Then golf cart around
On our beautiful place.

I love these moments.
They are precious to me.
Can't think of anywhere
I would rather be.

As I grow older
And she does, too,
These granddaughter days
Are priceless — it's true!

October 14

Making Dill Pickles

Making dill pickles
Is so much fun,
Working in the kitchen
Until they are done.

Hearing the pop
As each jar seals.
A feeling of satisfaction —
What a thrill!

But even greater
Is when we get to taste
The work of our hands.
Not a pickle will go to waste.

We'll remember the fun
On a Friday night.
Making dill pickles:
What a delight!

October 15

BIRTHDAYS

Birthdays come so quickly
When age creeps in.
But, oh, the joy we feel,
Celebrating with friends.

It has been said,
Age is a matter of the mind;
If you don't mind,
Then leave our age behind.

I can truly say
I don't mind birthdays at all.
I truly love to reminisce
On the ones I had when I was small.

And now that I'm much older,
I can stand and say
I am truly thankful
For each and every day!

October 16

Flood-Proofing Life

There is going to be a flood,
Jesus warns us time and again.
A day we will stand before God
To answer for all our sins.

What levee will we have ready
When that day appears?
Will it be our profession of faith
As that time draws near?

We say, "I believe in Jesus,
I received Him in my heart.
When I was just a child,
I gave Him a little part."

"I didn't give Him all.
I thought just part would do.
But I realize now
He needed all of me and you."

Some will try the levee of pride.
They have faith in themselves.
The Cross to them seems useless;
Into His Word, they never delve.

October 16

There is a remnant practicing
To understand God's Holy Word.
They truly devote themselves.
His will for them is heard.

So when the impending flood comes,
Before God in judgment we stand.
What levee will we use?
Will it be the Son of Man?

October 17

Time Alone

We all truly need
Some time alone, I say,
To think about the things
Important to us today.

Is it what we'll wear,
Or maybe what we'll eat?
Is it who'll win the game,
Or who will feel defeat?

Is it a time to worry
About all the "could-have-beens,"
Or give it all to God
And feel true peace within?

That's just what I'll do,
Just put it in His hands.
He's the great Creator
Who really understands

Time alone!

October 18

Happy Fiftieth, Son

Today's an awesome day,
For fifty years ago
God allowed me to give birth
To an awesome son, you know.

Those months that I carried
Him so near my heart
Are engraved in my memory,
Where they'll always be a part

Of who I am.
For a mother I became
To a precious baby boy.
John Dennis (J.D.) is his name.

I thank God on high
For the privilege to say
Happy fiftieth birthday
To my son today.

October 19

Baking with a Friend

Tonight was very special.
I went to bake with a friend.
Sharing, laughing, talking
From beginning until end.

Our husbands were so gracious.
They took a little ride,
And came back with pizza
With a salad on the side.

Her house smelled so delicious,
Pumpkin roll and pecan pies.
What a joy it is!
They turned out great … surprise!

Baking with a friend,
You should try it and see
Just how much fun you'll have,
Like my friend and me.

October 20

Harvest Moon

The harvest moon,
Shining so bright
As it illuminates
The dark of night.

Its golden glow
Gives a special air
To warm our souls,
Knowing God is there.

And He is watching
From heaven above,
Showering us with peace
And joy and love.

Just as the harvest moon
Illuminates the sky,
Lighting our way
From the heavens so high.

October 21

Relief from the Heat

The wind is blowing;
There's a chill in the air.
Fall has arrived,
Leaves scattered everywhere.

Acorns cover the ground,
Crunching under your feet.
Little squirrels scurry,
Gathering some to eat.

Mums are in full bloom,
A colorful array.
Swamp daisies, tall and proud,
In the strong winds sway.

As the temperature drops,
We are grateful today
For relief from the heat
That is coming our way.

October 22

Enjoying God's Gift

We awoke this morning
To see many limbs on the ground.
So after breakfast and Bible study,
To work is where we were found.

Together we worked diligently
To get the task over and done.
The yards looked so great,
And working together made it fun.

We love this land we own
By the help of God Almighty.
He's allowing us to enjoy it,
And I don't say that lightly.

We are so very thankful
That we can work this land.
We have learned to appreciate
All we've been given by God's hand!

October 23

A Fork in the Road of Life

There comes a time
When a fork in the road
Stands before us
Like a heavy load.

All who reach it
Must make a choice.
The broad or the narrow:
One leads to sorrow, one to rejoice.

One way leads to heaven,
The other way to hell.
Which road will you follow?
Have you failed

To follow God
In your life's span?
When you come to the fork,
Will the Father reach out His hand?

If you follow the majority,
How sad will be your fate.
You've followed the wrong road,
And it is too late

October 23

To enter God's kingdom.
Obedient you must be,
For the grace of God
Sets all people free.

There's a fork in the road;
Eternity there awaits.
The broad or the narrow:
Which will be your fate?

October 24

Live According to the Word

Lord, help us live
According to Your Word.
Through Your mighty grace,
Let Your voice be heard.

With Your Holy Spirit,
Guide us day by day.
Help us understand
You are the truth, the way.

You treat all our problems.
You listen, and You hear.
Each complaint You know
Before we ever draw near.

You alone fight for us,
Keeping the devil at bay.
We just have to call Your name;
You make temptations go away.

Father, make us attentive
To Your Word, I pray.
For Your Word is life;
We need to live it day by day!

October 25

The Gospel Message

The Gospel message is powerful;
Its Words from God on high.
It's the "Old Time Religion";
It's as good as apple pie.

When we look at today's generation,
All the technology that abounds,
We often think these "know-it-alls"
Don't even know their way around.

But God loves these millennials.
We should love them, too.
We should reach out to them,
Give the Gospel message true.

For this Gospel message is powerful;
God is still welcoming souls.
We need to work in the fields,
Where His message needs to be told.

October 26

SEASONS OF LIFE

Just as the year has seasons,
We have seasons of life, too.
Spring, summer, fall and winter
Are seasons we go through.

In spring, we are born;
In summer, growing day by day;
In fall, we continue to mature;
In winter, we're well on our way

To being all we can be,
For old age has crept in.
Our youth has slipped away.
That's the fate of all men.

But life is precious still.
Always remember, God knows best.
And at the end of our winter season,
To believers, God promises rest!

October 27

So Many Blessings

As we awoke this morning,
There was a golden hue.
As we looked out the window,
There were no skies of blue.

As the sun began to rise,
Those golden hues turned gray.
We speculated to ourselves,
What would be in store today?

An early breakfast with coffee,
A few chores for us to do.
After our daily Bible reading,
A couple of calls and texts, too.

Then get dressed and decide
How the rest of our day would go.
Lots of busyness as usual;
So many blessings. God, we love You so!

October 28

A Together Day

Today has been
A together day,
From beginning to end
In work and play.

Sharing the load,
Whatever it may be.
Working side by side,
For eternity.

How sweet to walk
Hand in hand,
Just being together
Is, oh, so grand.

I love together days,
Praying for many more.
Can't wait to see
What God has in store!

October 29

THE MOUNTAINS BECKON

The mountains beckon
Us to come
See God's beauty,
The mountains to roam.

See the leaves,
Their beautiful hues,
Browns, greens, yellows and oranges,
Even purples, too.

As you climb,
You see valleys below.
You say to yourself,
"Which way should I go?"

As the mountains beckon,
You answer the call.
Spending the day there
In October's fall.

October 30

A Glorious Day

It's been a glorious day
From beginning to end,
A worshipful experience
That truly transcends.

A beautiful sunrise
To start the day,
To warm the body and soul
In a special way.

Then in the evening
When sunset falls near,
Its magnificent colors
Start to appear.

Reminding us how blessed
To have such a glorious day
To begin a new week,
For whatever comes our way.

October 31

TRICK OR TREAT

Ghosts and goblins,
Princesses and kings
Run door-to-door
And doorbells ring.

Hoping there'll be candy
Or some special treat;
Never a trick,
But something sweet

To put in their bags
On Halloween night,
As they scurry in costumes,
Watching for witches in flight.

Trick or Treat,
When the night falls.
Watch out for the children,
One and all!

November 1

Exciting News

There's nothing like
Hearing your grandson say,
"You're going to be a great-grandmother
Again in April or May!"

Not just with one,
But baby twins;
A whole new adventure
Soon to begin.

The joy in his voice,
The love on his face,
These are priceless moments
No one can erase.

We pray, Heavenly Father,
Bless this couple as we share
This very exciting news
With this precious pair!

November 2

Roosters Crowing

I hear the roosters crowing,
"Get up and start your day;
There is so much to do.
In bed you cannot stay."

Just outside your door,
The world does await.
So hop to it, friend;
Get up and meet your fate.

I bow my head in prayer
And thank my God above
For trials and for blessings
He gives to me with love.

Again, the roosters crow,
Beckoning the morning to begin.
I chuckle to myself,
"They're saying, 'Get up, God's ushered a new day in!'"

November 3

Fall Feels Like Summer

Fall feels like summer
On these very warm days.
When we're looking for cool air,
It seems to have gone away.

The sun is beaming,
The grass turning brown.
Leaves crunching under foot
All over the ground.

Rain is truly needed,
But none is in sight.
The plants are starving;
They look a fright.

Please come, fall weather;
Summer needs to go.
We need some heat relief;
Cool weather, make a show!

November 4

Great News

Today we got great news.
Someone we hold dear
Got great news:
It wasn't cancer, as he feared.

We bowed in thankful prayer
For this gift divine.
One of God's miracles;
His love continues to shine.

What a wonderful day
To share with family and friends,
This great news
From beginning to end!

November 5

Precious Family Time

Family time is precious.
We never know when
One of us won't be here,
And it won't be. Then

We'd say to ourselves,
"Wish we had done more
To spend time together."
If we'd only known before

That time would be short,
We'd try harder, too,
To be together more often.
That's what we should do.

For family time is precious;
May we cherish every one,
And make our time together
Lots and lots of fun!

November 6

Troubled Times

Lord, we are living
In very troubled times.
The world is spinning,
But Your people are out of line.

Rapes, murders, meanness abound,
Nothing new under the sun.
You are, and always have been,
The only perfect One.

Please forgive Your people.
Let Your mercy and grace flow.
There is still that remnant
That depends on You, You know.

So, in these troubled times,
My strength and courage be;
Let my light shine
Continually for Thee!

November 7

The Sky Tonight

The sky tonight is brilliant,
The moon and stars shining bright.
The wonders of the universe
Are such a glorious sight.

An airplane zooms up high,
Rushing to its next destiny.
Many people in a hurry
To get from A to Z.

I love looking at the heavens
Where God's majesty abounds,
The beauty of the sky,
And the earth that it surrounds.

I bow my head in awe
At the beauty of the sky,
To thank my Heavenly Father,
Living far above on high.

November 8

Dusk Is Here

As I look out the window,
There's an orange glow all around.
Dusk is here so quickly;
Darkness shortly is found.

What happened to the daylight?
Those twenty-four hours flew.
Time surely passes quickly;
There's so much yet to do.

The sun in the western sky,
Giving off its glorious hues,
Saying, "It's time to settle down."
Saying, "Rest" to me and you.

For dusk is here, dear ones,
The night quickly ascends.
Close your eyes and sleep,
A new day will quickly begin.

November 9

Red Sky

At two o'clock this morning,
I saw a very red sky.
I knew it was an answer to prayer.
I gave a relieved sigh.

I should not be surprised;
I've seen it time and again.
The Master of the Universe
An answer always sends.

I felt a wondrous peace
Down deep in my soul.
Oh, the glory of His majesty
I once more behold.

Thank You for the red sky,
For always being here,
Deep within my heart,
My Savior, My Lord, so dear.

November 10

Gone, But Not Forever

Today a precious lady
Will be laid to rest.
While she was living,
She gave her very best.

A godly life she lived,
An example to one and all.
With her quiet spirit,
Her faith stood very tall.

All who knew her will miss
Her gentle, precious hugs.
The way she truly cared
At your heart strings tugs.

The beauty of her presence
Not seen on earth again,
But with the reunited
A glad reunion will begin!

November 11

Silent, Loud Whispers

Have you heard
The silent, loud whispers
From God above
Sent to you in love?

They may not be audible
Except to you.
These silent, loud whispers
That ring true.

You know of creation,
But do you understand?
God made it all,
Even human man.

Do you hear the whispers,
Whether awake or asleep?
Some silent, some loud,
Yours to keep.

November 12

INWARD ... OUTWARD

Where does beauty lie,
In the soul or outside?
True beauty from within
Is where radiance begins.

For if the heart is pure,
It shines for all to see.
From inward, it goes outward,
As illuminating as can be.

Mother always said,
"Beauty is skin deep,
Ugliness to the bone.
Beauty may fade, ugliness holds its own."

So seek for inward beauty,
And outward it will flow,
Letting the world know for sure
The reason you seem to glow.

November 13

Idol Worship

It's not just golden calves
We idolize today;
It's the things of this world
That cause our hearts to stray.

It might be our children
Or our husband or wife we adore;
It might be our money
Or our need to explore.

It might be a Cadillac
Or a souped-up Ford;
A mansion on a hillside,
Or a drink we've poured.

It may be a cell phone
Or a computer, too,
That becomes our idol,
Yes, of me and you.

So people realize anything
Can be an idol, my dear;
So be very careful, friend,
For only God is entitled to hear:

November 13

You are worshipped.
You are adored.
You are praised.
Forevermore!

November 14

Super Moon

Tonight, there shines
A super moon.
So big and beautiful,
In the heavens it looms.

It has been
A long, long time
Since this moon
Has shone sublime.

Its orange glow,
Giving the sky
A brilliant hue
That seems to cry,

"Enjoy me now
While I am here;
I won't be back
For many more years."

November 15

SMOKY HAZE

Our land is covered
With a smoky haze.
Wild fires are prevailing
These last few days.

Our earth is in danger,
Burning forests galore.
Lord, we need You;
Open heaven's door.

Send down the rain.
Put the fires out.
We know You're in control.
We praise and shout!

Take away the smoky haze
So we can breathe free.
Thank You, dear Father,
For hearing our plea!

November 16

Christmas Decorations

I love this time of year,
Christmas decorations galore,
The excitement of the season,
Looking forward to what's in store.

Bright lights shining,
Trees decorated in finest array,
Just in time to celebrate
The coming of Christmas Day.

Christmas carols playing,
Peace on earth to all men.
What a wonderful blessing,
Such a great feeling within.

How wonderful it is
To honor Jesus' birth,
Singing "O Little Town of Bethlehem"
With joyous mirth!

November 17

Evening Quickly Comes

When the time changes,
Evening quickly comes.
It seems the sun rises,
And before you know it, day is done.

We scurry during the day,
Doing all we can,
Before the evening comes
And darkness starts to descend.

The warmness of the day
Wanes into the coolness of the night,
As families settle in,
Cutting off the lights.

For evening quickly comes
When fall sneaks in,
And time changes
Once again!

November 18

Making Memories

I love making memories
With the ones I love,
Spending the day together,
Hoping there will be more of

Days just like this one,
Laughing, talking, such fun;
Just being together,
Enjoying the beautiful sun.

Riding on the golf cart,
Eating lunch together, too,
Doing a little shopping,
Things we like to do.

Making precious memories
To cherish in my heart,
And recall at any time
When we are apart.

November 19

First Freeze

The first freeze of the season
Is on its way tonight.
Flannel sheets on the bed,
And we're snuggled up real tight.

I'm enjoying the cooler weather;
The summer was so hot,
It's time for a break.
I really like this weather a lot.

We have the water dripping,
Don't want the pipes to freeze.
All the flowers are in the barn,
Praying that the trees,

Deep-rooted, will survive
And blossom in the spring,
When warm weather comes around
And birds begin to sing.

November 20

Redeeming the Insignificant

God, our Heavenly Father,
Redeems each and every one.
It doesn't matter how insignificant;
He gave His only Son.

We should never underestimate people,
Or think they are less than we.
For all are very important
To the Lord, you see.

The power of God in us
Is a weapon against our flesh, too.
God can destroy strongholds
When the devil tries to lure me and you.

Lord, our churches have potential;
We need to release now.
He redeems the insignificant;
Watch Him at work. Wow!

November 21

Pickle-Making Time

It's pickle-making time again,
And it is so much fun,
Working in the kitchen together
Until the process is done.

Each one has a part
In carrying out the plan
In making our dill pickles;
Pray they turn out grand!

Some of the greatest memories
Come from simple pleasures like this:
Our family being together,
Times I'd sure hate to miss.

Looking forward to more moments,
More pickle-making times, too.
Having fun in the kitchen:
One thing I love to do!

November 22

Making Snowmen

I am making snowmen,
But they're not made of snow.
They are bottles I'm recycling,
Made of plastic, you know.

Each one is unique,
Each has a smiling face,
Each one sitting on a shelf
In its special place.

I look at them and dream
Of real snow, where I can make
A true snowman figure,
Not one that is fake.

But for now, I'll enjoy my snowmen
And share them with family and friends,
Until winter comes, and just maybe
We'll have real snow … God sends!

November 23

All Day in the Kitchen

All day in the kitchen,
Cooking for a feast.
That's what tomorrow will be,
To say the least.

Families coming together,
Celebrating Thanksgiving Day.
Parades and football games:
That's the American way.

The house smells so wonderful:
Holiday scents galore.
That's what a day in the kitchen
Always has in store.

Tired? You better believe it!
But it will be worth it all,
When we sit down to eat
And say, "Dig in, you all!"

November 24

THANKSGIVING DAY

Today is Thanksgiving Day:
A time for family to share
A wonderful meal together
And show how much we care

About making memories
That last a lifetime through,
And thanking God, our Savior,
For all the blessings given to you.

Family from far and near
Gathering this time of year,
Feasting on all the goodies
Filling our hearts with cheer.

Then each family leaves for home,
Kisses and hugs all around,
Wishes for a Merry Christmas,
Praying for blessings to abound

On Thanksgiving Day!

November 25

Shopping Spree

Today we went on a shopping spree;
It was so much fun.
We four girls were looking
For that special one

Gift to please someone we love,
To put under the Christmas tree —
And then to watch them open it
And see them filled with glee.

Shopping is usually a chore
That I really don't enjoy to do.
But it was really great today;
I truly felt real joy, it's true!

The four of us together,
On today's shopping spree,
Was such a super treat
For them and for me!

November 26

Quiet Day

Today has been
A quiet day,
A day to reflect
And then say,

"What a great week
This has been,
From Sunday's start
To Saturday's end."

Visiting with family
This holiday week;
Good food, good fellowship,
Can't be beat.

Then to top it off
With a quiet day.
What could be better?
"Nothing," I say!

November 27

My Two Favorite Men

Started the day
With my two favorite men:
God, my Savior, and
Kirby, my best friend.

Reading the Bible,
Bowing to pray,
Thanking our Lord
For another day.

Then getting dressed,
Off to church we go:
Kirby in one direction,
Me another, you know.

Back together for lunch,
Then once again
Back to our respective churches
We travel when

It's time for choir practice,
Bible study, too;
This is our routine
On Sundays we do.

November 27

We are so blessed
God uses us this way.
Playing Christian music
Makes this a special day.

And just like my day started,
It, too, will also end.
I'm a very joyful lady
With my two favorite men.

November 28

A Busy Lazy Day

Today has been
A busy lazy day,
Doing things I love to do:
Some work, some play.

Cooked a pot of mustard greens,
Decorated more of the tree,
Put some things up outside;
Looking more like Christmas to me.

My heart filled with joy,
Thinking of times past.
When my grandchildren were small,
Christmas was always a blast.

Lord, thank You for memories
And for busy lazy days,
Doing things I love to do,
Whether work or play.

November 29

THIS HOWLING WIND

I lie here quietly
Listening to the howling wind,
Hear the leaves falling,
Praying rain will begin.

Days and days of drought,
The land is thirsty and dry.
Wildfires growing daily;
We need rain to satisfy

The parched ground begging
For a little relief,
So very dusty and thirsty
Above and beneath.

The dark clouds flying quickly
To another destiny,
As the howling winds subside,
And the earth cries, "Please rain on me."

November 30

A Walk Through the Woods

There's nothing like
A walk through the woods.
Exploring fall's nature,
The brisk air feels so good.

There are leaves covering the ground,
Hickory nuts everywhere.
Animal footprints,
Birds flying here and there.

Skies of steel gray,
No sun in sight;
The threat of rain
To fall before night.

A walk through the woods,
Clearing your mind.
And you never know
What you might find.

December 1

SUPPER WITH FRIENDS

There's something special
About supper with friends.
Laughing and talking,
Voices that blend

With joyous tones
Of the season's delight,
Just being together
On this December night.

Discussing our day
And the days ahead,
In this very busy month
That lies ahead.

So tonight we'll have fun
From beginning to end,
Starting off having
Supper with friends.

December 2

Movie Fun

Today was a day
To have movie fun
With great-granddaughter Kellie
After dinner was done.

The movie was "Moana,"
Cute as it could be,
Especially special
With Kellie sitting next to me.

Oh, how I love
Making memories sweet,
Having movie popcorn
As a yummy treat.

Praying for more days
To have movie fun
With my great-grands
Before my life is done!

December 3

Shopping Date

Starting out early
For our shopping date,
Then arriving home
Really late.

But, oh, the fun,
Pop right by me,
Searching for gifts
To put under our tree.

Tired feet, weary joints,
Spirits floating, we journey home.
Enjoying the decorations;
We're surely not alone.

Traffic flowing speedily,
Yet the beauty of the Christmas lights
Warms our very souls,
Ending our shopping date — such a delight!

December 4

Rainy Day

Rainy day has come,
We're as thankful as can be.
Seems it has been so long
Since it rained, you see.

The earth was so thirsty,
The leaves had turned brown;
The streams running low,
So delighted rain has come around.

The Father always knows
Just what His creation needs.
So He sends a rainy day,
For He has heard our pleas,

Asking for the rain
To fall from the sky above,
And refresh the earth
With His wondrous love.

December 5

All I Want for Christmas

All I want for Christmas
Is a happy family,
Gathered all together
Around a lighted tree.

Although that seems impossible,
I think of years gone by
When we were so much younger,
But, oh me, oh my …

Our family is now scattered,
Each has its own, you see.
It's hard to gather them all
Around that lighted tree.

So this year, all I want for Christmas
Is my memories to be clear,
As I look at all the pictures
Gathered over many years.

December 6

God Is More than Santa Claus

God is more than Santa Claus,
More than tinsel on a tree.
God is our salvation,
Hung upon a tree.

Once Santa seemed important
When I was just a child,
Until I learned of true Christmas
Born in a baby, meek and mild.

I learned how He could change me,
Forgive me and so much more.
I learned all I have to do
Is open up my heart's door,

Receive Him as my Savior
And grow with Him each day.
For God is more than Santa Claus:
He is the Living Way!

December 7

CELEBRATE LIFE

Today was a day
To celebrate life, my friend,
A gathering of many
So we could attend

The celebration
Of a precious soul
As she was laid to rest,
And to behold

Memories held closely
To all those there
Of the times
We had to share.

The love she showed
Throughout her life's span;
A true celebration of life
When she was born … began!

December 8

I Blew My Diet

Today I blew my diet,
When out to eat with friends,
Had those peppermint pancakes
I knew were a diet sin.

But, oh, they were delightful,
Each and every bite.
I tried to tell myself
It won't hurt for just one night.

The scales were not so kind.
They said, "My, oh me.
You've gained almost a pound."
"Just a pound?" I said with glee!

Okay, I blew my diet,
But tomorrow is another day.
I'll just have to exercise
To take that pound away!

December 9

BRRR! IT'S COLD OUTSIDE

The sky is a brilliant blue,
The sun is shining bright.
But, *brrr,* it's cold outside!

There is frost on the car windows,
The chickens snuggling close.
Because, *brrr,* it's cold outside!

But we are warm and toasty
Thanking God for our heat.
Yes, *brrr,* it's cold outside.

We feel so excited
This season of the year.
Even though, *brrr,* it's cold outside.

The coffee so delicious,
Warms us up really quick.
Brrr, it's cold outside!

December 10

Bride Again

One day, I'll be a bride again;
The Bible tells me so.
Not like I was on earth,
But someday I will go

To where my groom is waiting,
His arms open wide,
Where I will live eternally
With Him to abide.

He'll take me by my hand
To explore our beautiful place,
Where I will see loved ones
Of every creed and race.

What a joyous wedding day
When I'll be a bride again,
Living with the One
Who washed away my sin.

December 11

Leap for Joy

There is a reason
To leap for joy,
For the Father sent
A baby boy

Into this world
Filled with sin
To save the souls
Of sinful men.

Oh, how wondrous
Was the sight
Of the stars
That shone that night.

Today we, too,
Should leap with joy
And thank our Heavenly Father
For His Baby Boy!

December 12

All Days Are Precious

The day started out
Bleak and forlorn,
Fog all around
On this early morn.

No sunshine in sight
For most of the day,
But we continue traveling,
And as we do, pray

For the sunshine to break
Through the drab clouds,
Giving a new perspective
As God allows.

All days are precious,
Whether sunny or bleak.
There's always a silver lining
If we just seek!

December 13

Aunt Linda's Place

This morning we're sitting
At Aunt Linda's place.
Feeling warm and cozy,
Thinking of God's grace.

Look out the window
And what do we see?
Deer moving about,
Roaming safe and free.

A squirrel hustles down
A tall oak tree.
Looking for acorns,
Sees us, then flees.

What a glorious morning
To sit quietly and share
The wonders of nature
We see everywhere!

December 14

Remembering Can Be Painful

Remembering can be painful,
Cutting you to the bone.
But in these times of sadness,
You realize you're never alone.

There is a mighty Father,
Watching from up above,
Who sees your tears
And showers you with love.

He walks beside you;
He is always there,
Sharing in your sorrow
With tender, wondrous care.

Though memories are painful,
There are good ones, too.
So reach down deep in your heart;
Allow God to strengthen you!

December 15

You Opened a Door

In the wee hours of the morning,
When darkness seems to prevail,
There's no light to be seen,
Yet, the Father never fails

To bring sweet comfort
When our world falls apart,
And we seem to be bleeding
From a truly broken heart.

It's then on our knees
We begin to earnestly pray.
Help us to see clearer
At the dawning of day.

Give us strength to go on,
As You have so many times before.
For when You close a window,
We realize You opened a door.

December 16

Wooden Christmas Wagon

The wooden Christmas wagon
I bought so long ago
Holds many memories
Of the grandchildren pulling it to and fro.

They take out all the characters
Within the wooden door,
And put them around the wagon
As they lie on the floor.

I listen to them talking,
Their sweet voices clear,
And wonder what they'll be doing
In the next few years.

Each year as I take out the wagon,
I remember all the fun back when
The grandchildren were playing with the Christmas wagon
On my floor once again.

December 17

CHRISTMAS MOVIES

I love watching Christmas movies,
Could sit for hours on end.
Some of them so old,
I've seen them again and again.

But I never get tired
Of watching them once more,
For most of them are joyful,
Making Christmas spirits soar.

Some are animated;
Some are black and white;
Some of them so funny
You giggle half the night.

Precious Christmas moments,
Especially with family.
Watching all those movies
With my loved ones next to me.

December 18

Exchanging Gifts

Exchanging gifts
Is so much fun,
Wondering if
You purchased the right one

For every person
On your Christmas list.
Will it fit?
Do they insist

It was what they wanted.
How did you know?
Their happiness
Just seems to glow.

A sigh of relief,
You bought the right thing.
Oh, the joy
Exchanging gifts brings.

December 19

My Sister's Birthday

Today is the day
My baby sister was born.
What a beautiful gift,
Six days from Christmas morn.

The picture of health,
So fragile and sweet.
I was so excited,
I felt my heart leap.

I could hardly wait
For her to grow,
So I could teach her
Some of the things I know.

This day will always be special,
Whether she's far or near.
This beautiful Christmas present
God gave me that year.

December 20

Priceless Ornaments

I have many priceless ornaments
Hanging on my Christmas tree.
Each one has a special memory,
Especially those given to me.

There have been so many,
And each could tell a tale
Of times we shared together,
Of love that never fails.

There are snowmen and angels,
Bells and turtledoves;
Ones made by grandchildren,
Filled with all their love.

Lights that shine so brightly,
Giving these priceless ornaments a glow,
Reminding me how truly blessed
By those who've loved me so.

December 21

SADNESS, GO AWAY!

At this time of year,
Joy should truly abound.
But in some households,
Sadness seems to be around.

The passing of a loved one,
The separation of families;
Many people homeless,
No joy do they see.

We pray for peace on earth;
We greet passersby,
Not knowing their situations.
We've come to realize

We don't want sadness.
So, Lord, please take it away.
Replace it with true joy.
It's almost Christmas Day!

December 22

MY CHRISTMAS VILLAGE

In a corner of my living room,
My Christmas village is on display.
I keep it up all year-round;
I look at it each day.

My family has given me pieces,
I treasure each and every one.
Sharing it with others
Is truly so much fun.

There's a church on the top shelf.
It's the most precious, you see,
Reminding me of my Savior
Who died to set me free.

Oh, how I love my Christmas village,
Each piece selected with care,
And left out on display each day
So its beauty I can share.

December 23

The Little Things in Life

I truly miss
The little things in life,
Like the curiosity of a child:
Why can't I play with a knife?

Why do people snore?
Why can't I go outside?
Why must I wear a hat?
Why is it bad to lie?

All the "why, why" questions
They ask every day,
The little things in life
That quickly slip away.

I miss those whys;
I miss the curiosity of a child.
So I cherish those sweet memories.
Remembering makes me smile!

December 24

TWIN GIRLS

Our hearts are overflowing.
We're great-grandparents, you see.
Soon there'll be twin girls
In our expanding family.

Two more precious babies
For us to show off with pride.
Our happiness is bursting
Deep down inside.

We ask for God's protection
As they daily grow.
Protect their precious mother,
For Father, we know

Seth and Jessica will be great parents.
They will shower these girls with love.
They will teach them of you
Living in heaven above.

December 25

Christmas Day

It's Christmas Day once again,
So different than when
Our children were young
And their anticipation began.

When they would rise to see
What Santa left under the tree:
Toys, bikes, dolls and trains,
Hoping it surely wouldn't rain

So they could go out to play
And become exhausted before the end of the day,
From rising so early to see
What Santa left under the tree.

As they grew up, they realized
That the greatest gift of life
Was celebrating Jesus' birth,
God's only Son sent to earth.

That Christmas Day is so much more
Than they ever imagined before,
That "peace on earth, good will to men"
Was sent in the form of a babe, then

December 25

Grew up and died upon a tree
On a lonely hill called Calvary,
Rose to life and in heaven lives.
And salvation, to us, gives

If we receive Him in our heart,
So when we die He can impart
Eternal life forever to be
Celebrating Christmas with Him, eternally!

December 26

Exchange and Buy

Today is a day
To exchange and buy
That Christmas gift
That made us sigh.

We thought it was something
We couldn't live without,
Not anything at all
Like it was advertised about.

Exchange lines so long
We could hardly see,
The end of standing
Seemed like an eternity.

Gift cards, gift cards,
The way to go.
They can buy what they want.
No disappointment, you know!

December 27

A Night with Friends

There is nothing like
A night with friends.
Grabbing a snack,
Then conversations begin

How was your day?
What did you do?
Did you see the grandkids?
What else is new?

Do you remember?
Sometimes no, sometimes yes.
It's so much fun
To just reminisce.

Nothing could be better
Than a night with friends.
A nightcap of coffee,
A perfect day's end.

December 28

Taking Down Our Tree

Soon the decorations
Will be put away,
Packed up neatly
For another Christmas Day.

The lights and glitter
No longer will shine,
Except in our hearts
And in our minds.

This most precious season
We all can attest
Is so very special,
One of the best!

So, slowly we take down
Our Christmas tree,
Cherishing each ornament
Made for you and me.

December 29

Sunup to Sundown

From sunup to sundown,
We're busy as bees.
Moving from place to place,
The day to seize.

There is so much to do,
So many people to see.
Some work, some play
For you and for me.

It seems like the hours
Quickly slip away,
From the dawn of morning
To the end of day.

From sunup to sundown,
Father, help us to be
Found faithful and true
For eternity!

December 30

I Wonder What Lies Ahead

I look out the window
As the sun begins to rise.
The sky is a brilliant red,
And I wonder what lies

Ahead as dawn turns to morning.
What will the day have in store?
What message is God sending?
What will I explore?

I bow my head in praise;
I have another day
To give Him thanks,
And to humbly say,

"Give me strength and courage.
Let everyone I meet know,
Like the red sky in its beauty,
Let my love show."

December 31

ANOTHER END

How wonderful it was
To bring 2016 to an end,
With some of our family
And very generous, loving friends.

There have been many changes
In these past 365 days,
Some of them delightful,
Some of them we wish away.

But God has blessed us,
Got us through each event.
His mercy and grace
He truly always sent.

So as we reach another end,
We pray for another day.
As we usher out 2016,
2017 is heading our way!

Epilogue

Seth,

As 2016 ends, I pray you enjoy this poetry, written especially for you. The year 2017 has so much in store for you — twin girls to bring you so much joy. I pray that each day will hold a new, exciting adventure for you, Jessica and your baby girls. I will always cherish my days with you, and I pray that God will allow me to live to make memories with your girls. I love you more than words could ever express!

GaGa

CPSIA information can be obtained
at www.ICGtesting.com
Printed in the USA
FFHW022037170619
52996267-58621FF